What Others /
About This

Spiritual Journey: Can I Really Get Close to God? is an expression of Dr. Wanda Walborn's heart for helping individuals experience the liberating love of God by identifying and eliminating obstacles to intimacy with Him. During a season, when I wrestled with discovering my purpose, Dr. Walborn walked alongside me as I processed my darkest secrets and hindrances to believing and receiving God's love for me. My life has never been the same. Dr. Walborn invites the reader to experience transformation from the inside out to gain a deeper relationship with God. She is well-equipped to empower and equip others based on her personal practice of the same disciplines she asks her reader to consider. Intimacy with God is a lifelong journey. Expect to encounter Him in fresh new ways through the practical steps presented in this important and life-changing book.

—**WANDA VELEZ**, *Vice President of Student Development and Dean of Students, Nyack College*

Reading words written by someone who lives her words and practices with integrity is a rich gift. The ancient image of "integrity" came from crafty potters who inserted a substance into cracked or broken pots and then glazed over the broken parts. To have integrity is to offer something that is whole from start to finish, no cracks, nothing covered over. I have been blessed to know this author, Wanda Walborn, for many years: as colleagues, trusted friend, and co-laborer for the sake of the kingdom of God. Her words are to be trusted; her insights are to be taken in and will bring growth and wholeness as they too are lived with the integrity she brings to her ministry. Don't just read this book: absorb it, metabolize its truth and live it

—**DR. KEITH ANDERSON**, *President Emeritus,*
The Seattle School of Theology & Psychology

Dr. Wanda Walborn has a unique style of communication which combines a pastoral tone with an underlying prophetic impulse. You are immediately drawn into a place of desperation as Dr. Walborn paints a picture of life immersed in deep intimacy with Jesus. The invitation is so compelling that I found myself physically leaning forward wanting more. The genesis of her writing, however, is in the practical call to deep personal reflection described as "mirror moments." It is in these strategic places of "holy pause" that the Spirit animates and heals our soul, removing roadblocks and opening pathways for genuine encounters with Jesus. The powerful and refreshing articulation of "spiritual disciplines" as friends or companions that make space for God's presence in our lives is brilliant. Intimacy is not about formulas but rather formation that is birthed out of perpetual encounters with the presence of Jesus. This book is not optional. Let the journey begin!

—**REV. DR. DAVID HEARN**, *President of the Christian*
and Missionary Alliance in Canada

Wanda is a trustworthy friend and ministry colleague, a woman of depth, wisdom and insight who is a reliable guide on the Spiritual Journey. Take the trip with her through the inner life and stop along the way to look in the mirror and allow the Lord to take you to new places that you need to experience for freedom and fullness in Christ!

—**DR. ROB REIMER,** *Associate Professor of Practical Theology at Alliance Theological Seminary and author of* Soul Care

"...those who are close to Him are those who are desperate for Him..." "As uncomfortable as desperation is, it is the gifted reminder of my need for a Savior to save me from myself. My yes is the doorway for change and transformation." "On a scale of one to ten...how thirsty are you for more of God?" These quotes from Dr. Walborn's book describe the reason why one would read this book and journey with her through the process and soul-shaping patterns towards spiritual formation, wholeness, and freedom. There are key principles here that will help shape the life of any believer—whether you're just beginning the journey in your walk with God, or you've been on the journey for a long time but are hungering for more; more intimacy; more of the depths of His love; more of Him! Dive into *Spiritual Journey: Can I Really Get Close to God?* She dives in with you and leads you on a journey to spiritual breakthrough and getting intimately close with God.

—**REV. KELVIN L. WALKER,** *District Superintendent of the C&MA Metro District*

Walborn captures the essence of spiritual disciplines as the "grace to make space for God's presence in our lives." She contends that to live authentically is nothing less than the fruit of God's grace, received and given. This book is biblical and practical, born from a life of faithful discipleship and fruitful ministry, and will offer rich insights into your own spiritual journey.

—**GRACE MAY,** *Associate Professor of Biblical Studies,*
William Carey International University
and Founder of Women of Wonder, Inc.

From the mature Christian to those simply curious about spiritual matters, those brave enough to allow Dr. Walborn to guide their journey will find themselves uniquely equipped to discern the voice of God and to enjoy the rest that comes from sitting in his very presence. Of all the spiritual disciplines, those explored within this text are perhaps the most elusive, but most necessary for spiritual lives free of fear, anxiety, burdens, and shame. Dr. Walborn knows that in the presence of Christ exists abundant grace and complete freedom. She is journeying to that sacred place and this book is her invitation for you to come along.

—**SHIRLEY HOOGSTRA J.D.,** *President,*
Council for Christian Colleges & Universities

I have watched my wife, Wanda, pursue Jesus for over 36 years. It's one of the reasons I fell in love with her. I had never met anyone with such a pure, intense devotion to encountering God. Her pursuit inspired and motivated me. In "Spiritual Journey" Wanda shares many of the secrets and obstacles she has learned and faced along the way. Her insight is deep and refreshing. I have watched her live it. This book will give you a glimpse into it as well. I believe Wanda's journey will inspire you as it has me. Our prayer is that you would enjoy the journey into His presence as much as we have. It's worth it!

—**Dr. Ron Walborn**, *Vice President & Dean, Alliance Theological Seminary and Nyack College*

I've known Wanda for two decades as a professor, colleague, coach, and friend. I've watched her emerge into a leader of influence and insight. This book integrates the best of human development with insight into the Scriptures. Her perspectives on brokenness, fear, and shame are stellar. I commend this work to you.

—**Dr. Martin Sanders**, *President & Founder, Global Leadership and Director of Doctor of Ministry, Alliance Theological Seminary*

Spiritual Journey:

Can I Really Get Close to God?

Dr. Wanda Walborn

Carpenter's Son Publishing

Spiritual Journey:
Can I Really Get Close to God?

© 2020 by Wanda Walborn

Published by Carpenter's Son Publishing, Franklin, Tennessee

Published in association with Larry Carpenter
of Christian Book Services, LLC
www.christianbookservices.com

Edited by David Brown

Cover Design by Hyler Fortier & Kelly Walborn

Cover Photo taken in Spain on El Camino de Santiago by Wanda Walborn

Interior Layout Design by Suzanne Lawing

Printed in the United States of America

978-1-952025-20-4

Dedication

To my husband, Ron

It has been my great joy and honor to walk this journey with you for the last thirty-six years. Thank you for choosing me. God knew exactly what He was doing when He put me with you, because you love me so well. You know when to press in and you know when to give me space. You speak truth directly, and even though at times, it hurts, it is always needed—not initially well-received, but needed. You make me laugh so hard and you have no trouble sharing your feelings. You have made room for me in ministry when you didn't have to. You gave up your spot countless times so I would keep developing. You believed in me when I didn't believe in myself and you wouldn't let me hide behind you. You are the love of my life and there is no one I would rather journey with than you! I love you.

Contents

Foreword

One hundred seventy-five years ago, sitting in a cabin constructed by his own hands near Walden Pond, Henry David Thoreau wrote, "The mass of men live lives of quiet desperation." It was his literary critique of the general malaise he saw in the society of his time. As he observed, people were not in touch with the deepest longings of their lives, settling for a form of existence far less fulfilling and exciting than the adventure for which they had been born.

In some ways, little has changed since then. People are still experiencing a relentless gnawing in their souls, craving to experience a "more" that they seem incapable of discovering or even describing. I suppose, though, one thing has changed since Thoreau penned those words. The desperation is no longer quiet. The cry for love and significance has become almost deafening, as men and women turn to performance, people pleasing, privilege, possessions, and power, exhausting themselves in fruitless efforts to find meaning that ultimately leave them broken and empty.

The more astute, like Wanda Walborn, know that what we need most is to be loved unconditionally, forever secure in the embrace of the One who is love Himself. That is why she wrote this book. It is inviting us to turn toward the Gentle Voice that beckons, "Come to me and you will find rest for your soul."

If any book ever deserved a warning label, this is the one. The cover should read, "Caution, reading this will take you on an adventure that will forever change your life." I must tell you that the focus of this resource is far more than conceptual or informational. Make no mistake, there are profound insights here, as well as the integration of sound psycho/spiritual principles. But *Spiritual Journey* goes far beyond the mere interesting to the episodic. It will engage your senses and affections in such a way as to draw you into the deep where lives are forever transformed. Reading this will birth a vision of what could be, of what should be the very purpose and significance of life itself.

Walborn's integration of experiential learning will birth a deep awareness of God's movement in the present moment of your life, which is her definition of the process of spiritual formation itself. The exercises of reflection found in what follows will draw you away from the clutter and busyness of shallow existence into the richness of intimacy with God, bringing a confidence that when you cry, He will come to you with love.

I encourage you to say yes to the adventure contained in the chapters ahead. Even more so, I recommend Wanda Walborn as your guide. Yes, she is a proven and experienced educator, spiritual director, and pastor. But more than that, and what encourages me most about her, is that she is a Wounded Healer. Wanda Walborn guides with vulnerability and honesty. It is with love and openness that she describes the peaks and the valleys that comprise the journey into God's embrace. There is sweetness in these pages, but no sugarcoating. There is encouragement, but no pretense. *Spiritual Journey* is the real deal, and reading it is an investment you cannot afford not to make.

Terry Wardle
Professor Emeritus of Practical Theology
Author of several books, including *Identity Matters* and *Some Kind of Crazy*

Preface

YOUR ADVENTURE
INVITATION

This book answers the gnawing question, Can I really get close to God? Whether you're a new seeker or experienced traveler, the spiritual journey is broken into bite-sized pieces so you can understand God's heart for you and respond to His invitation of love. You will learn to hear His voice and break through barriers that block your attempts for closeness. Few books show you what to do when you get in God's presence. Provided Mirror Moments and Practices allow you to pause and look in the mirror to reflect the window of your soul to see what God might be saying to you. Saying yes to God provides the pathway through the obstacles to His loving embrace.

What do you love? For me, one of my favorite things to do is travel. I love to go, go, go, and am up for any adventure! Seeing new sights, eating different foods, meeting new people, and exploring new trails are all part of the excitement. After a great trip, I love to talk to one of my closest friends with the sole purpose of convincing her to come with me next time. Since I now know what to expect, I can give her a heads-up about what to pack, what time of year to go, and how much money to bring. I highlight my favorite parts of the trip, including stories of things I know she loves, so she will say yes to my invitation to come. My goal is that she will be so sold on the idea that by the time I'm done talking, she is ready to book the trip so that she can experience some adventure for herself. The same is true for you and for this book.

Are you ready for a spiritual adventure?

Every journey comes with some adventure. No matter how well we plan for any trip, something unexpected always happens. Part of the fun in life is not knowing what could be waiting just around the corner. Me, I have been on a spiritual journey with God for almost fifty years. He has taken me to mountaintops and through deep, dark valleys. As with any adventure, I have favorite spots I frequent and other places I hope to never return to. I've walked with many, many people throughout years of church ministry in Connecticut and California. I have journeyed with many students at Nyack College and Alliance Theological Seminary in New York City, so as you and I prepare to go on this God adventure together, I know some really cool spots to show you along the way. I share very personal stories so you can understand that I'm not asking you to do something that I haven't struggled through myself.

Some things will make you uncomfortable, some things will stretch you, and some things you won't even think you believe, but I am asking that you come anyway and try anyway. My prayer is that you will experience a new or refreshed closeness to God that you've only dreamed of. There is no time frame for completing this journey. I, too, am still on it. Give yourself the grace to go at your own pace and linger if necessary. I will keep giving you loving nudges to keep you going so you don't get stuck or drop off the trail once it gets hard. Some of the best lessons learned are when we are exhausted and have a very bad attitude. I assure you that every blister, rash, and sore muscle you encounter along the way is worth it.

I can see the skepticism on your face. You may be leery of my enthusiasm because you have been promised things in the past that eventually faded. This is different because I am going to teach you to go to God by yourself and for yourself. Why? Because then you won't always need me to translate. I'm going to share with you how to hear God's voice and give you time to be alone with Him in Mirror Moments. During these times, God will make you aware of obstacles blocking your path. In some cases, you've lived so long with fear, rejection, anger, unforgiveness, and rebellion that you aren't even aware they are barriers. You think this is just the way life is and this is as good as it gets. That is a lie from the enemy. There is more, so much more of God to be found on this spiritual journey.

After you discover and remove those roadblocks, we will then discover the way through each one. Once you know what they are, I will share with you suggestions to keep them out of your life, but it will take practice for you to adopt a new mindset and create new habits that will ensure you have the tools to walk in your newly found freedom.

God desires for each of us to have a loving and intimate relationship with Him. If you have always longed for that, or if you are ready to get back to that special place, then I just have one last question for you. Have you packed your bags yet? There's so much more joy and peace for you to experience on this spiritual journey. Grab your bag, lace up those shoes, and let's go!

WANDA WALBORN
May 4, 2020

Acknowledgments

There are countless people to thank when it comes to this project. I must start with Mom and Dad, Carol and Larry Haggerty, for being the first people to introduce me to Jesus and the spiritual journey. Thank you for loving the Lord and each other without apology!

To Ron, Kelly and Anthony, Brice and Megan, Karis and Petey, and Karly and Josh for always being up for new adventures. You are always the first ones I want to share a new part of the journey with. Not a day goes by that I don't think of you and pray for you as you walk your own spiritual journeys with the Lord. You know His voice, so keep drawing near to Him, and do what He says. I love you.

To Kelly Anne for encouraging me for years to finish this book and create a website. "Get out there!" I think is how you said it. Well, dear, here it is! Thank you for nudging me.

To Bella, Ashton, Hayley, and the grandchildren yet to come. You have always been in the back of my mind as I have written this, with the prayer that someday you would choose to step onto the path and follow Jesus wholeheartedly for yourselves. Nana loves you very much!

To Hyler for doing your friend Kelly a favor to help out her mom with the cover design. Thank you for putting up with me changing my mind so many times.

To Heather for faithfully serving with me at Nyack College, where this book marinated inside me for many years. You saw this book long before I did. You have been a loyal friend for many years, praying for me, listening to the Lord with me, encouraging me, brainstorming with me, asking me clarifying questions, reading chapters, giving helpful feedback, helping me format Word documents—ugh!—and reminding me countless times that an editor would tell me if something needs attention. Thank you for believing in me.

To Lisa, Amy, and Wanda for being my safe place to process my own spiritual journey for so many years.

To Mike and Lisa for being my pastors for over fifteen years. Thank you for your friendship.

To my editor, Tiarra, for your insight and perspective and to my publisher, Larry, for your professionalism and genuine care as you walked me through this process.

To Terry for writing the foreword. Your healing journey opened the door for me and many others to begin our own healing process. Thank you.

To Tracy for your invaluable insights and encouragement to help me find my voice.

To all the students of Nyack College and Alliance Theological Seminary for daring to step onto this journey and give yourselves to the Lord when you thought I was crazy to ask you to sit in stillness, then record what God said. It is a joy to journey with you!

To my Empower Leadership Team: Becky, Val, Kim, Heather, Catherine, Lisa, Ashley, Melissa, Rachael, and Amy for journeying with me as we lead Empower. Your butt-kicking ability to get stuff done is inspiring, and I love bringing the Kingdom with you!

To the women of Empower for trusting me to introduce the journey to you and for you to courageously step onto the path. I know I scared you at times, and my nudge felt like a push, but you said yes to God and He changed your lives. Let's keep going and bring His Kingdom to many other women!

To Jesus for putting in my heart the desire and longing for more of you. I love you.

Chapter 1.

PREREQUISITE FOR THE SPIRITUAL JOURNEY: DESPERATION

The secret of spiritual success is a hunger that persists ... It is an awful condition to be satisfied with one's spiritual attainments ... God was and is looking for hungry, thirsty people.[1]
—Smith Wigglesworth

Can I get closer to God? People frequently ask this question with hopeful anticipation of a magic formula to follow that will do the trick. They want to know God but don't understand that those who are close to Him are those who are desperate for Him. Nothing else satisfies their longing for love like Jesus. When we think about those whom Jesus healed, they were those who had no other place to go. They had tried everything. They spent all their money on possible solutions, only to come

---

[1] http://archives.relevantmagazine.com/god/13-smith-wigglesworth-quotes-will-challenge-your-faith#VGjQ7dhbIcIc5G09.99

up empty. What did they all have in common? Their desperation drove them to Jesus. Each one laid at Jesus' feet the hope
of being healed, and He looked on them with compassion and
healed them. It didn't matter what the ailment was. Lepers,
the blind, the lame, the deaf, and parents of dying children all
came with the hope that He could and would help them. Their
longing, their hope for something better, and their faith were
the impetus for them to seek Him out, no matter what anyone
else thought or said of them. They had to get to Him, and they
would do whatever it took to reach Him.

DO YOU LONG TO BE CLOSER TO GOD?

Relentless desperation is not new. Newborn infants have it
too. I know you can't go back far enough in your memory to
recall when you were newly born, but all your needs were met
because of your relentless desperation. When you were born,
you were small and vulnerable. Your automatic response to
all things was to seek the comfort of your mother or caregiver. That reliance was brand-new. Imagine yourself lying in
your bassinet with everything around you bigger, louder, and
brighter than anything you had ever experienced. You rely on
your caregiver for every need. You can't walk, talk, or even
hold up your head. The only thing you can do to communicate
is cry. Whether rooting for your mother's breast or producing
a high-pitched bloodcurdling scream, your desperation for
food, touch, closeness, or affection is met by your cry. There
is no manual, so your caregiver seeks to determine what you
need. Are you cold, hot, hungry, soiled, tired, angry, or do
you just want to be held? Imagine being a helpless creature
who can't do anything for yourself. You have lived inside your
mother's body for nine months while growing and being

soothed by the rhythmic beating of her heart. You have only known warmth and safety in the confines of her womb. Your whole life has been comforted by the sound of her voice and the movement of her body.

Then everything changed. Can you imagine yourself in that place? From warm fluid to cold air, darkness to piercing light, muffled sound to extreme loudness, and worse, from hearing her heartbeat every single moment to missing its rhythm. Cry? Of course, you cry. Even that is new. For the first time, you are able to utter a sound, and you happily discover that if you do, she will come. She will pick you up and hold you close, pat your back, kiss your head, or gently bounce you up and down, assuring you that everything will be all right. Do you want to be picked up? Yes. Do you only want her? Yes. Do you long for the way it used to be? Yes. You cry to return to the arms of the One who knows you and protected you as you were being formed. Her heartbeat was the measured metronome that comforted you. All you have to do to find her in this new world is to cry with all your might. This instinct to cry is all you can do to make known that you want her. You need her. You are desperate for her. She has been your dwelling place, refuge, and hiding place. She is all you have ever known. The security of her body has been your sanctuary, and you cry, not only to find her again, but to experience the comfort and peace that is only known in her arms.

LONGING FOR LOVE

The longing an infant displays for a caregiver is similar to the longing we have for God. The longing for closeness, tenderness, safety, and love is instinctive in all of us. We were made from love, formed in love, and require love for healthy growth and development. The magnitude of need behind an infant's cry cannot be dismissed. Denial of basic needs in vulnerable moments will not teach the lesson of secure individualism. It will do the opposite. By letting a baby cry, the first lesson learned is that no one is coming. That lesson is reinforced until the child wrongly concludes, "I am not worthy of love." They learn that those around them are not capable of loving them, because their cry solicits no response.

Attachment theory legitimately reveals that when our needs have not been met adequately as infants, we learn to repress our desire to love and be loved. We have an expectation that we will not be heard or cared for, so we don't bother to ask anymore.[2] Russell Moore, in his book *Adopted for Life*,[3] describes going to an orphanage in Russia as he and his wife were in the process of pursuing adoption. The silence from the nursery was eerie. The babies in the cribs never cried. Not because they never needed anything, but because they had learned that no one cared enough to answer.

Children who are confident in the love of a caregiver cry.

Children who are confident in the love of a caregiver *cry*.

[2] J. Bowlby, Attachment and Loss: Vol. 1 (New York: Basic Books, 1969); J. Bowlby, *Attachment and Loss: Vol. 2, Separation: Anxiety and Anger* (New York: Basic Books, 1973); J. Bowlby, *Attachment and Loss: Vol. 3, Loss: Sadness and Depression* (New York: Basic Books, 1980); see M. D. S. Ainsworth, "The Development of Infant-Mother Attachment," in Review of Child Development Research, eds. B. M. Caldwell and H. N. Ricciuti (Chicago: University of Chicago Press, 1973), 1–94; M. D. S. Ainsworth, M. Blehar, E. Waters, and S. Wall, *Patterns of Attachment: A Psychological Study of the Strange Situation* (Hillsdale, NJ: Erlbaum, 1978); J. P. Allen, C. Moore, G. Kuperminc, and K. Bell, "Attachment and Adolescent Psycho-Social Functioning," Child Development, 69 (1998): 1406–1419.

[3] Russell Moore, *Adopted for Life* (Wheaton, Crossway Pub, 2015).

Unfortunately, some of us have made the same conclusion about God. We believe He won't come to us. The result? We cry out less and less. We have cried out in the past, seeking solace in our distress, and He didn't respond the way we expected, or as quickly as we would like. In some cases, He didn't respond at all. Despite the strong exterior that we painstakingly maintain, we desperately want to be held, soothed, and comforted, but continue to be met with silence. Our experience of loneliness and detachment, in spite of our longing, doesn't connect with the message that God loves us and wants to be close to us. It's as if we are on two different parallel planes that will never intersect.

When we stop and answer, with brutal honesty, these two questions, "Am I worthy of love" and "Are others capable of loving me," it reveals our belief or disbelief that our need for love can be satisfied. Attachment to God theory shows that the answer to these two questions indicates the outcome as secure, fearful, anxious, or avoidant in adult relationships.[4] At the core of our being is an innate longing for love. From the very beginning, before we could even speak, we learned whether or not it was safe to express our need and ask for help. What we learned as infants is reflected in our deeply engrained belief system. Our response to this belief system inhibits or enhances our ability to draw near to God.

---

[4] L. A. Kirkpatrick and P. R. Shaver, "Attachment Theory and Religion: Childhood Attachments, Religious Beliefs, and Conversion," Journal for the Scientific Study of Religion, 29 (1990): 315–334; K. Bartholomew and L. Horowitz, "Attachment Styles Among Young Adults: A Test of a Four-Category Model," Journal of Personality and Social Psychology, 61 (1991): 226–244; L. A. Kirkpatrick, "God as a Substitute Attachment Figure: A Longitudinal Study of Adult Attachment Style and Religious Change in College Students," Personality and Social Psychology Bulletin 24 (1998): 961–73.

If you struggle with drawing near to your heavenly Father, I challenge you to embrace the mirror moment below. These mirror moments allow you to pause and reflect the window of your soul to see what God might be saying to you.

As children of God, we can approach God's throne of grace with confidence so that we may receive mercy and find grace to help us in our time of need (Heb. 4:16). God is present. He promises to answer before we call and hear us while we are still speaking (Is. 65:24). His eyes are ever on us and He is attentive to our cry (Ps. 34:15). It will take persistence on our part to keep coming to God despite the lingering fear that He may not respond. We must push past this nagging fear and come anyway. He is faithful and He will come to us.

Mirror Moment

Take a moment to answer these two questions. Don't give what you think is the right answer. What do you *really think*? Your honest answer is the starting place for drawing near to God.

Am I worthy of love? Yes or no, and Are others capable of loving me? Yes or no.

If you answered **yes** to both, you lean toward **secure** relationships, believing that you will be heard when you ask for help.

If you answer **no** to both, your negative view of self and others causes you to be **fearful**, thus avoiding relationships, believing no one can be trusted.

If you answer **yes** to am I worthy of love and **no** to are others capable of loving me, you tend to be **avoidant or dismissive** in relationships. You often hold people at arm's length, believing you must be self-reliant.

If you answer **no** to "Am I worthy of love?" and yes to "Are others capable of loving me?," you are often **anxious** in relationships, believing that because you are not worthy of love, others will tire of loving you and abandon you.

OBSTACLE: REFUSING GOD'S LOVE

Are you ready to grow? Acknowledging and accepting our brokenness is the starting place for any and all who begin the spiritual journey. Shame has robbed us of the truth of who we are and that we are loved as we are. Shame's message screams that we are broken, worthless, unlovable, forever tainted, useless, and defective. Grace's message is one of hope, forgiveness, and love. The empowering presence of God comes to us, despite our doubts, providing a way for us to return to His unending and limitless love. God whispers in our ear that it is okay not to be okay. Why? Because Jesus' sacrifice of love makes us okay before the Father. He goes on to assure us that this sacrifice was done out of love, for love, with the hope that we would choose to live in this love. Receiving such a gracious gift can only be lived out through faith, because the exchange is highly disproportionate. Past and present sins were the reason Jesus had to die in the first place. He willingly came to earth to make a way for us to return to intimacy with the Father. He knew the sacrifice was worth it—that *we* were worth it—to go through such pain and agony so we could live in freedom. Indeed, it is a disproportionate exchange.

LET ME LOVE YOU

His invitation is simple. Let me love you. It is a short and sweet statement that rocks our world and quickly brings all things clearly into perspective. No power, wealth, or fame can manipulate its way into possessing salvation. Instead, it is extended as a simple invitation to be accepted or rejected. Whoever you are, whatever you own, or wherever you live doesn't matter in the least. The offer is extended to us all.

"Will you let me love you?" It is a powerful question causing many to be undone emotionally upon hearing the proposal. On the basis of this offer, we can live the life we were created for—a life of loving response to the One who made us. A loved person is secure in his or her identity. A loved person lives out purpose and destiny with joy. A loved person brings others along for the ride, knowing the Father will accept them too and make room for them at the table.

"Will you let me love you?" Skeptics warily look out of the corner of their eye to find the catch to such an offer. Our human nature has taught us that everything is transactional. When it sounds too good to be true, it usually is. God's offer of pure love is overwhelming. We have learned to bargain for things, because we have only experienced conditional love with hidden motives. Skepticism gives way to cynicism, and our attention is turned toward all the professing Christians who have ever hurt us. The pain is too much to bear because we trusted once and were burned by the very ones who bear Christ's name.

"Will you let me love you?" When we answer that question, it's easier to say that we tried and His people (those Christians) hurt us, so we slam shut the windows and doors of our souls. We secure our walls and reinforce the barricade around our hearts to protect ourselves from answering this vulnerable request. We look beyond the people who hurt us to God and blame Him for our pain. We replay in our minds our flawed understanding of His sovereignty. "He put me with these people, knowing this would happen. He allowed them to hurt me anyway." Some of us will go one step further in this line of thinking to say out loud that we don't think God is good. An admission of this sort would reveal being a "bad" Christian (tongue in cheek) who doesn't trust God to work all things together for good (Rom. 8:28). We cannot blame God for what people have carelessly or intentionally done to harm us. We can't blame His sovereignty for the actions and choices others have made. Our faulty deductions borne from our painful experience dictate our continued state of imprisoned loneliness. We turn away from the only one who truly knows the depth of our need and can meet that need in full with His love.

JUST AS I AM

I want us to recognize something critical to our under-standing. This offer to let God love us is not about other people loving us. This offer is about allowing ourselves to let God Himself love us in a naked and unashamed kind of way. The thought of our nakedness before God is what brings shame, causing us to turn away from such an offer and cast our eyes to the ground. It's one thing for us to know that God knows everything, but it is quite another thing for us to be complete-ly bare before him.

It is a natural reaction to feel shame when we bring our dirt (the theologically correct word is sin) to God. It doesn't com-pute in our minds that He would love us as we are. We have been trying for years to scrub off this dirt by our good deeds toward others, giving money to the church, or volunteering at places of need. The thought behind such actions is that if we try hard enough, work hard enough, or prove ourselves enough, God will love us. Once again, the offer has nothing to do with what we can accomplish or produce. "Will you let me love you?" is a plain and simple offer.

We are given the choice to allow someone to lavish His affection on us. It's a simple offer with extraordinary results. We are given what our heart longs for by simply receiving this generous gift. It's as if someone has been watching our lives, knowing we need someone to cover us. The offer is given, and instead of accepting the free gift, we insist that we don't need the handout. "No thanks. I'm all right. I'm good." Pride wins out and resolve rises up from within to prove our ability to live on our own.

> Accepting such a profound, yet simple, offer of love is an act of humility because it is an admission of need.

Accepting such a profound, yet simple, offer of love is an act of humility because it is an admission of need. It is an admission of weakness. It is an admission that says, "I am not okay as I am." It is in this place that the Father scoops us up in His arms, hugs us tightly, and whispers in our ear, "Beloved, it's okay that you aren't okay. I will take care of you."

As we allow ourselves to feel the emotion of His love holding us, we become undone in our emotions. Years of unresolved pain and pent-up emotions rise to the surface and can only be expressed through sobs of relief. The resistance is over. The fight is over. All the self-rejection and self-hatred, or self-righteousness and pride are released through our tears and we now have room for that love to reside in us.

AS MUCH AS YOU NEED, YOU GET

The best part about this is that it's not a one and done. As much love as we need, we get. It's not an annual reception or quarterly, monthly, or weekly deposit. It is meant to be lived in daily in a moment by moment encounter in His arms. When we have a moment of weakness, fear, insecurity, doubt, or pain, we simply call out to Him and He is right there to give us more of Himself. He who is Love (I Jn. 4:8, 16) has entered into relationship with us, so we never have to be without it. The phrase from the old Beatles song "All You Need Is Love" is true. When we experience love like this, we begin to live differently. We become more courageous. We become more adventurous. We become more secure in our lives and our faith. We are free to be who God created us to be, and we now want to seek His guidance to learn what that is.

Through this journey of realizing God's love, we learn that there is no need to compare ourselves to others. Gaining confidence in who we were created to be increases our awareness of how the enemy uses comparison to create a divide between us, God, and others. We will experience that being ourselves is all God wants. It is enough. We will see firsthand what great love the Father has lavished on us that we should be called children of God! And that is what we are (I Jn. 3:1)! Will you let Him love you?

THE WAY THROUGH: DISCIPLINE OF YES

The ongoing response to our desperation for love is by saying yes to God's invitation to love us. Accepting God's gift is the easy part. Living in that love is a discipline. We will have to fight through doubt until our experience matches our knowledge that He is with us and for us and on our side. Accepting God's love is a choice we must make every day. We commit ahead of time to say yes, so we won't weasel out of our commitment later when times get hard and we don't feel like sticking with it.

Spiritual disciplines are a means of grace whereby we come to God to seek greater intimacy with Him. Participating in these disciplines is an act of humility. It is a sacrifice of ego when admitting the need for help outside ourselves. Coming to God by participating in these disciplines gives Him permission to change us. Many times, I have made a mess of things and I come in desperation to seek help, God's help, by giving my life to Him. Saying yes to God is therefore the first spiritual discipline to be practiced, because left to myself, I will default to demanding my own way.

Saying yes to God is a continuous act of submission to relinquish my will to be in control. A predetermined, unequivocal yes is an indication of love and trust in Him. By giving up the choice to say no ahead of time, my repeated yes is a pledge to live a life of willing surrender to God. Hearing the request ahead of time and making a decision based on what is best for me in the moment is no longer my first choice. God is now in control, and I yield to His will for my life. I don't know what lies ahead. I don't know what I will be asked to do. I don't know where I will be asked to go, or even if I will like it, but my decision has been made. I will say yes to God. Why am I willing to make this definitive decision? Simply put, I know, trust, and love the person who is asking.

I don't know about you, but my track record for getting myself into trouble is pretty extensive. God's track record for showing up on my behalf is perfect, so I say yes again and again. His way has always been the best, even when I couldn't always tell it would be from the beginning. There is a depth of trust in the relationship with love as the primary reason for saying yes, much like a best friend or spouse asks for something and receives an unhesitating, immediate response of yes.

As uncomfortable as desperation is, it is the gifted reminder of my need for a savior to save me from myself. My yes is the doorway for change and transformation.

A work colleague once stopped by my office to ask for a favor. Without explanation, he said, "Will you do me a favor?" then paused and waited for my response. After a considerable length of time, I replied with a big smile and a joking tone, "Well, it depends on what you want. I need to know what you want before giving you an answer." He laughed and proceeded to tell me what he wanted me to do. It felt manipulative that he started with the ask, when he could have just as easily started with the context of the situation, then made the ask. As it turned out, I happily chose to assist him with what he needed, but an ask requires relationship.

THE CHOICE

Saying yes is a choice, but like any relationship that holds value, it is a daily choice to love. Saying yes to God means there is deep devotion belonging to no one else, because of the release of one's heart to another. The writer of the Song of Songs 4:9 indicates that the bride has ravished the bridegroom's heart by a glance of her eyes, but he is equally delighted and responsive to her presence. This level of vulnerability comes with the promise that all will be given for the other. Jesus demonstrated his love for mankind by giving his life. Our responsive yes demonstrates the giving of our lives in return.

FEAR OF MISSING OUT

Accepting God's gift of grace and forgiveness doesn't mean we will always make the right choice. The first potential roadblock to saying yes to God is the fear of missing out. Choosing one thing limits options. The possibility that something better might come along is enough to make us question our commitment for a wait and see attitude. What if there is someone better? What if this doesn't work out? What if I'm not good at it? What if I don't like it? The desire to leave things open-ended causes more stress than a decision, because there is no certainty that something better will come along.

What ifs that rule a person's life leave the outcome as choosing to live in a state of liminality. There is only a possibility or wishful hope that someone or something better *might* come along. The other side of the coin is equally a possibility in the what if stance. What if this is the love of my life? What if this is exactly what I wanted? What if this is the best thing that has ever happened to me? Commitment is a guarantee of my daily choice as I willingly live out my decision to love. By closing the door to all options, my focus is clear to wholeheartedly devote myself to my choice. Both my head and my heart play a role. My heart feels love and my head commits to daily honoring the choice. Feelings come and go, but in those times, my decision to love carries me until the feelings return. True love replaces infatuation and superficiality.

In all relationships, as in all new things, eventually disillusionment sets in. A crossroads is faced to either veer from the commitment or hold steady. Will you choose to keep your commitment or will you look for something better? If there has not been an adequate grieving of losses—loss of freedom and loss of options—the greater the desire will be to run away. The most common thought that surfaces during such times is that this is not what I thought it was going to be like. Revelation of this kind leaves you reevaluating your original decision. Reality versus fantasy leaves you needing to choose again. Do I stay or go? Am I in or out? Do I say yes or no? There is always a choice. Always. And we live out our choices.

PRIDE

Another roadblock to saying yes to God is pride. The right to be independent is abandoned by a posture of humility. What I want, when I want it, or with whomever I want is laid on the altar by my choice to depend upon another person for everything. Control demands sight and understanding, but faith is unseen, embraces ambiguity, and surrenders to the will of another person. Choosing to live a life of surrender eliminates the thirst for power and recognition. Pleasing the masses is replaced with pleasing the One. Saying no to all others increases the value of the yes. In choosing God, the way of dependency has been chosen. The way of the servant. The way of the unknown and unseen. Dependency feels weak and vulnerable, because dependency is vulnerable. Fully trusting that you can rely on another person is risky. It can seem like a stupid, irresponsible thing to do, but allegiance of this kind is a beautiful picture of childlike faith. Reaching out in faith to receive the gracious gift offered by Christ is the appropriation of Jesus' request, "Do me a favor, say yes."

PRACTICE: PRAYER OF INTENTION

If you are ready, take a moment to tell God of your willing-ness to try to say yes to Him in every area of your life. Even the wording of "willingness to try" indicates that saying yes is a choice. I'm sure you have very good reasons for not wanting to trust God. Will you push past those reasons and try? Before praying, ask God to show you areas where you protect yourself from Him. Your yes opens the door for His entrance into your life.

Dear God, I say yes to you in the area of my _____ _____, which is the most difficult place for me to trust you. I know I need love, so I say yes to you now.

Please come and show me that you are real.

DISCUSSION QUESTIONS

These questions are intended to be shared in a small group setting. Being part of community is also a part of the spiritual journey to have other people listen to us, support us, encourage us, and challenge us.

1. *How would you describe your hunger for God? Are you more like the infant searching for his mother, or the infant in the Russian orphanage? Explain.*

2. *What response rises up in you when you read this verse: "The eyes of the Lord are on the righteous, and his ears are attentive to their cry"?*

3. *How often do you compare your weakness to someone else's strength?*

4. *What are your answers to the mirror moment questions: "Am I worthy of love?" and "Are others capable of loving me?" How accurate is the conclusion that you are secure, fearful, anxious, or avoidant in relationships?*

5. *What prevents you from letting God love you?*

Chapter 2.

SPIRITUAL JOURNEY: WHAT IT IS AND WHY IT'S IMPORTANT

*"But small is the gate and narrow the road
that leads to life, and only a few find it."*
—MATTHEW 7:14

Since I started my journey of trusting and saying yes to God, there has never been a dull moment. When you decide to join this journey, you will learn that it features more adventure than you could have imagined. The best part? God is looking for men and women in whom He can confide and share the secrets of His heart (Ps. 25:14). He wants you to walk with Him.

Drawing near to God reveals our true motives. We want a formula we can easily use to get close to God. We want the version of relationship heard about on TV that if we give our lives to God, then we will be rich and successful. All our problems will fade away and everything will be great! This version of relationship focuses on what we get from the relationship, rather than who we are with on the journey. The spiritual journey is not what we do or don't do for God. The spiritual journey is about traveling with the One we love to experience life together within each present moment. Our love for each other is deepened as we travel and we begin to catch a glimpse of our purpose for existence. We walk at our own pace to take in the view along the way, whether engaging in great conversation or silently embracing the beauty of creation. Each experience is something to be cherished as unique to our journey as each day unfolds.

BARRIERS ALONG THE WAY

At times, there are hills, boulders, cliffs, fallen trees, or annoying people who block our way. Only passion and perseverance provide inspiration to keep moving and remove obstacles. Temptation to quit is a common part of the journey, as weather conditions, length of the daily walk, sore muscles, aching feet, blisters, and rashes appear at the most unexpected times and places. Only travelers who value the relationship keep going, because only those who want more of God get more of God.

Some people like the idea of the journey, but don't want to put in the needed effort to train or get in shape for it. They just want to say they did the trek, not embrace every aspect of it as an equal part of the whole. Pain and joy are equally necessary companions found on the journey. You can experience both at the same time, and their presence often reveals wounded places in our soul that need time and attention for healing. The spiritual journey is a pathway available for anyone to join, but it is not for the faint of heart.

God desires to have a personal relationship with us, but wants us to choose intimacy with Him in return. God did not seek to have an intimate relationship with anything else he created, because no other part of creation had the capacity to love. We were created with the capacity to love deeper and deeper and deeper through relationship. We love because God first loved us (1 Jn. 4:19). We desire because God first desired us. We seek God because He first sought after us. Awareness of love is not sufficient. We were created for loving intimacy, which is a response to the whispers of longing put in our hearts by our Creator. We have been created first and foremost to receive the love of God and in turn love Him back through relational intimacy.

JOURNEY VS. DESTINATION

Your spiritual journey starts with intentional seeking of God. This journey is fluid and takes as long as necessary. There is no set destination on earth, only an assurance to be with God when our time here is over. The biggest blessing is what you see and experience along the way.

Spiritual pilgrimages are mankind's attempt to get close to God. By going to physical, sacred places as an act of religious devotion, we try to find a way to connect with God at a location or place believed to be holy. Mecca, Vatican City, Lourdes, Camino de Santiago, Char Dham, Tibet, and Israel are places where people make spiritual pilgrimages to meet God. Mankind is always seeking, but God is always drawing. Apart from God drawing us to Himself, we wander. The journey of spiritual formation is an intentional choice to draw near to God and become like Jesus. The apostle Paul spoke of

God's intentionality to create within each of us a desire to seek God when he spoke,

> From one man he made all the nations, that they should inhabit the whole earth; and he marked out their appointed times in history and the boundaries of their lands. *God did this so that they would seek him and perhaps reach out for him and find him,* though he is not far from any one of us. "For in him we live and move and have our being." (Acts 17:26–28a, italics mine)

God wants to be found by us. Jeremiah records, "'You will seek me and find me when you seek me with all your heart. I will be found by you,' declares the LORD" (Jer. 29:13-14a).

My father used to say, "You're as close to God as you wanna be." I think he said that to motivate me, but instead it struck fear in my heart that I could be closer and needed to try harder to do more for God to show Him I meant business. I interpreted the "could be closer" as "should be closer," so you "better get closer," rather than realize that God is the One who draws us in and His love is what keeps us close.

FOUR TYPES OF PEOPLE ON THE JOURNEY

You and I will meet various people on our journey. The first type of person on the spiritual journey is the theoretician, who is knowledgeable in theology and doctrine of many traditions. This person is very rules-oriented and law-abiding, believing that outward behavior is critical for acceptance by God. Relationship with God is more of a contract than a love relationship. The theoretician recognizes his need for God and decides to follow Him by believing the right thing and doing all that is expected. The theoretician has relationship from his head, whereby he hears truth, makes a decision to follow, and acts according to the system of that religion. The theoretician leans toward legalism because of its ease of application. Obedience to follow all rules will be followed without resistance.

The second type of person on the journey is the diagnostician, who judges others who do not know God the way he or she does. Personal experience, not the Bible, is the standard by which others are accepted or rejected. Arguments are a common occurrence with the diagnostician, because everything is based on personal opinion and must pass through the grid of his or her personal experience. Theological and doctrinal beliefs are shallow, or non-existent, because the focus is about following God *their* way. No other way is acceptable.

The third type of person on the journey is the observer, who is open to ask the question, "Is this God?" Style and form are not rigid; rather, there is an openness to find out if what is happening could be God's presence. This observer is looking for a relationship with God that surpasses duty and right behavior by adhering to a set of rules, and longs for love and affirmation with God and others. The observer is drawn by the attitude of others on the journey who are in love with God. The curiosity and hope that such a peace could be attained is attractive to the observer. There is a willingness to see if such behaviors and practices are helpful and pique the interest of the observer to search the Bible for answers and examples of such people and actions. The heart of the observer is open to be drawn into a deeper relationship with God like the psalmist who said, "Show me your ways, Lord, teach me your paths" (Ps. 25:4).

The fourth type of person on the journey is the practitioner. This person is open to trying new things, with the singular goal of intimacy with God. The practitioner is willing to try new ways of reading the Bible, prayer, and meditation to draw near to God. Suspicion and skepticism are not a part of the practitioner's mindset, because his or her relationship with God is already strong. Hunger for more of God causes this person to desire more of Him. Books, mentors, podcasts, sermon series, and Bible studies are all open avenues for growth and learning. The practitioner's posture is open and yielded to instruction by men and women of faith who are grounded in their beliefs about God.

Mirror Moment

Which one or two of these people on the journey do you tend to be like? Theoretician, diagnostician, observer, practitioner? Explain.

Would you be willing to try new things in your relationship with God as we begin this journey together? Your worldview will be stretched as you encounter new things.

DEFINITION OF SPIRITUAL FORMATION

Our working definition of spiritual formation is the intentional formal and informal process of giving God space in our lives to help us become like Jesus from the inside out to reflect the character of God, form a people of God, and participate in God's reconciling plan with mankind.[5] God's part is to do the

---

[5] Wanda Walborn, doctoral dissertation on "A Mixed Methods Study of Spiritual Formation: The Degree of Change in Grit and Attachment to God Among Ethnically Diverse Students at Nyack College," April 2015.

work. Our part is to give God space in our lives to do His work. We are changed at regeneration, which is why it is called the new birth, but we must choose to cooperate with God in the ongoing process. Kingdom living necessitates intention, effort, and even occasional difficulty, which is why spiritual formation is both a formal and informal process of giving God space in our lives. It occurs in formal training times like listening to sermons, reading books, and taking classes as well as through informal times of personal devotion, prayer, and conversations with friends. God brings opportunities for us to choose whether or not we will step into those moments to be changed a little more.

Our reflection of God (imago Dei), our formation through the church (ecclesiology), and our participation in the mission of God (missio Dei) give us purpose on the spiritual journey. Made in His image as the people of God, we have a unique mission to fulfill with Him to bring others back into relationship with Him. By giving God space in our lives, we become like another person. Our formation is not a set of rules and regulations to follow; rather, it is a process of becoming like another person through time spent together on the journey. We follow the person of Jesus, and through the development of our unique relationship on the spiritual journey, we begin to look, sound, and act like Him through the empowering presence of the Holy Spirit in our lives.

Imago Dei

The first purpose of spiritual formation was to make us aware that we reflect the character of God as children made in His image. This is called *imago Dei*. God wants us to love Him in return and have deep fellowship with Him, but without love as the motivation, our relationship becomes obligatory.

Dutiful relationships quickly become dull, predictable, and lifeless. Our eyes shift from loving Jesus to working for Jesus. And moving from relationship to religion. A love relationship never loses sight of the lover.

In our love relationship with God, we "find out what pleases the Lord" (Eph. 5:10). Such intentionality is exactly what happens in loving earthly relationships as well. Looking, watching, listening, asking, and noticing what pleases the other person is always on our minds because we want to go beyond saying we love them to showing we love them with our actions. This is what Jesus meant when he said, "If you keep my commands, you will remain in my love, just as I have kept my Father's commands and remain in his love" (Jn. 15:10).

Religion, on the other hand, is based on image and following the rules. It focuses on what a person does or does not do to earn God's love and approval, not realizing that we can never earn our salvation because Jesus already paid the price in full for our redemption (Heb. 10:10). As C. S. Lewis explains,

> Religion opens us to new possibilities of both good and evil. From that point on the road branches: one way leads to sanctity, humility, the other to spiritual pride, self-righteousness, and persecuting zeal. There is simply no way back to the mere humdrum virtues of the unawakened soul. If the Divine does not make us better, it will make us very much worse. Of all the bad men, religious bad men are the worst.[6]

As we respond in loving relationship to an all-powerful God who is at work in us, we have both the desire and power

---

[6] C. S. Lewis, *Reflections on the Psalms: The Celebrated Musings on One of the Most Intriguing Books of the Bible* (Orlando: Harvest Books, 1958), 32.

to do what pleases Him. God is not opposed to effort, as He tells us to "do everything with all our might and in the name of the Lord Jesus Christ" (Eccl. 9:10 and Col. 3:17). However, He is saying that our effort does not earn us more of God's approval and acceptance. God already loves us fully and completely in Christ and "we can only receive this gift by grace through faith" (Eph. 2:8).

James Ryle, one of the founding board members of Promise Keepers, defined grace as "the empowering presence of God enabling us to be all we were created to be and to do all we were created to do."[7] This definition puts the emphasis back on God's empowering presence as the source of our spiritual formation, not our effort. Made in the image of God, our lives are still broken and in need of our identity to be established in Christ through intimacy with Him. As we seek to become like Jesus, then we begin to reflect the character of God in our lives.

Ecclesiology

The second purpose of spiritual formation is to form a people of God. Spiritual formation is not meant to be done in isolation. In the Shema, it is clearly written that there is only one true God and He alone is to be loved (Deut 6:4–9). This was expanded by Jesus in Luke 10:27 when He adds, "And love your neighbor as yourself." This explicit inclusion of loving others is the introduction to missions, as it eliminates mankind's temptation to see religion as purely devotion to God. True growth can only occur as mankind is in relationship with one another. Theologian Darrell Guder rightly says,

---

[7] James Ryle, "God's Grace," sermon, Nyack College, Fall 2007.

The centrality of the community to the gospel means that the message is never disembodied. The word must always become flesh, embodied in the life of the called community. The gospel cannot be captured adequately in propositions, or creeds, or theological systems, as crucial as all of these exercises are. The gospel dwells in and shapes the people who are called to be its witness. The message is inextricably linked with its messengers.[8]

Our lives must speak louder than our words, since we are the representatives of the gospel message. Community fosters a sense of belonging, which is vital for accountability, fellowship, and healing. In true community, it is safe to share struggles with sin in order to receive encouragement and help in our relationship with Jesus. Belonging is very important in the body of Christ, and people must be able to come as they are to meet Jesus. God gave the church "gifts of leadership through the apostles, prophets, evangelists, pastors and teachers to equip God's people to do his work and build up the body of Christ" (Eph. 4:11–13) to be united in faith and mature in the Lord. God also intended "the church to be the manifold wisdom of God to make known the rulers and authorities in the heavenly realms" (Eph. 3:10), which is what we know as spiritual warfare. The church then "makes disciples of all nations baptizing in the name of the Father, the Son, and the Holy Spirit and teaching them to observe everything Jesus commanded" (Matt. 28:18–20). As the heart of God flows to the people of God, our performance and programs flow out

---

[8] Darrell Guder, *The Incarnation and the Church's Witness* (Eugene, OR: Wipf & Stock, 1999), 22.

of this relationship. This causes a deepened love for God and compels us to tell others about this loving God.

Spiritual formation flows best in the Community of the Beloved. Accountability, fellowship, healing, and community take place in this environment. People cannot hide when there is true fellowship, because there is vulnerability, honesty, and transparency regarding our personal brokenness. There is the recognition that healing comes through the body of Christ as we allow ourselves to be held accountable by others. This is not saying that we are to live with no boundaries; rather, it is an invitation to deep fellowship as we walk the journey of faith together. Reconciliation must always be on our heart to bring others back into relationship with God. This message of reconciliation makes us Christ's ambassadors (II Cor. 5:18–20).

Missio Dei

The third purpose of spiritual formation is to participate in God's reconciling plan with mankind. As the church, we are to be in the world, but not of the world to bring people to a relationship with Jesus Christ. The longer we are Christians, the fewer friends we have who don't know Christ. Part of this is due to our fear that the world will taint us.

According to M. Scott Peck, the two vices of fear and laziness lay at the very heart of sin. "Fear will keep us from practicing presence and proximity with non-Christian people, and laziness will keep us from regularly being in their world."[9] It is important for us to realize that our mission is simply to participate in God's mission incarnationally.

---

[9] Scott M. Peck, *People of the Lie: The Hope for Healing Human Evil* (New York: Touchstone, 1985), 45.

Missio Dei is the term used to describe the mission of God. As the church, we simply follow where God is leading us. Christopher Wright, in his book *The Mission of God*, writes of our relationship with God's mission.

> Fundamentally, our mission … means our committed participation as God's people, at God's invitation and command, in God's own mission within the history of God's world for the redemption of God's creation.[10]

God's mission is not simply to restore man's relationship with Him, but to also restore creation. Adam's fall affected the whole of creation, and the second Adam's redemption affects the whole of creation.

Prayer is a major way in which we participate in God's reconciling plan with mankind. We must seek the Lord to find out what He desires us to do. Prayer is the agency whereby God extends His kingdom, defeats Satan, and fulfills His plan upon the Earth. The Trinity is actively involved in fulfilling the will of the Father through prayer. As the children of God, we come to the Father to pray and ask for His direction, guidance, wisdom, will, purpose, or plan. The Trinity works in us to fulfill the will of the Father, in the name of the Son, by the power of the Holy Spirit. "For the disciple of Jesus, this stage of discipleship is not the first step toward a promising career. It is in itself the fulfillment of his destiny."[11]

---

[10] Christopher J. H. Wright, *The Mission of God: Unlocking the Bible's Grand Narrative* (Downers Grove: Intervarsity Press, 2006), 22–23.

[11] David J. Bosch, *Transforming Mission: Paradigm Shifts in Theology of Mission* (Maryknoll: Orbis Books, 1991), 38.

LOVE SEEKS ATTACHMENT

Our desire for God was put there by Him. Isaiah wrote, "My soul yearns for you in the night; in the morning my spirit longs for you" (Is. 26:9). The psalmist wrote, "My soul yearns, even faints, for the courts of the Lord," (Ps. 84:2) and "You, God, are my God, earnestly I seek you; I thirst for you, my whole being longs for you." (Ps. 63:1). Catherine LaCugna, Catholic theologian, explained God's yearning for us when she wrote,

> Our desire for God was put there by Him.

The deep yearning and desire for God we find inscribed in our hearts is more intelligible if that desire is rooted in the very nature of God, that is, if God, too yearns for and desires another, not out of need or lack, but out of plenitude of love... Love seeks attachment and affiliation, never fragmentation, solitariness, or autonomy. Divine self-sufficiency is exposed as a philosophical myth.[12]

In this view, God is attuned to and desires relationship with us. God wants to be close to us and is intricately involved in every detail of our lives. This is the definition of theism. He is not a god who set the world into motion, then left it to the natural laws of nature. That is deism. There are many Christians today who say they are theists, but live like deists, with no evidence of God's detailed involvement in their lives. In the evangelical church, it is preached that we have been made for

---

[12] Catherine Mowry LaCugna, *God For Us* (San Francisco: HarperCollins, 1991), 353.

God's purpose and He will mightily use us. No one wants to be used. We want and need to be loved. This journey of spiritual formation starts with love, because God is love (I Jn. 4:8), and we love because He first loved us (v. 19). If love seeks attachment and affiliation, God created us primarily for love.

In all religions, man is seeking God, but Christianity is the only religion where God came to man. Jesus came to Earth and became a human being to show us the way to have relationship with God in a very personal way. Jesus is the exact representation of the Father (Heb. 1:3), and since He died to pay for our sin, this gave us the opportunity to come back into relationship with the Father; we simply accept His invitation to join Him on this journey of relationship.

Mirror Moment

If and when you are ready, pray this prayer of intention.

Prayer: God, this is good news that you created me to have a love relationship with you. I want to do that, but I don't know how. I say yes to you and accept your offer to help me know you. Amen.

OBSTACLE: FEAR OF REJECTION

Hiding is common when it comes to relationships because it must first be determined if it is safe to really be ourselves. Do others want to know the real me? Can they handle knowing the real me? Will they accept the real me? Should I just play it safe and be superficial? I can be nice to them, smile, wave, hang out with them, laugh, and get pizza together, but will I ever let them know who I really am?

I once saw a book titled, *Why Am I Afraid to Tell You Who I Am?* I thought the answer was obvious. I am afraid to tell anyone who I am for fear of rejection. What you see is what you get, and if I am rejected, the result is being alone. The possibility of rejection is enough to put on a happy face and go with the flow. The decision is made to have no opinion about anything and let the other person choose the movie, type of food we eat, where we go, and what we do. Choosing agreement at all costs is the secret mantra of the person who fears rejection. The classic answer of such a person when asked anything is, "I don't know." The conclusion that coming off easygoing is much better than the risk of being known deflects all potential conflict or disagreement. It is not uncommon that over time, a slight depression will set in because of the incongruence. It takes far more energy to try to please others than to be known. What is the worst thing that could happen if you are known? Yes, rejection, but pretending is so tiring.

It takes time to decide one's viewpoint. Living so long without acknowledging thoughts and feelings requires time and space to discover what is there. Admitting it, naming it, and speaking it out loud will be another step to face the risk of rejection. It is in the very act of stating an opinion that self-discovery is found. Daring to say what we think indicates that we deem ourselves worthy to contribute to the conversation. A change of mind is also part of the process. Determining what we don't want is as crucial as determining what we do want.

Becoming friends with yourself is highly recommended before becoming friends with someone else. Lack of self-knowledge and acceptance leaves us open to taking on whatever persona is around, trying to get the acceptance we desperately long for as well as keeping the rejection monster from swallowing us alive and making our worst fears become reality. Differing from someone else is a good thing because it brings many facets to a situation to cover all angles. It is quickly learned that our particular way of seeing things is valuable to those around us.

REACH FOR THE MASK

Fear of rejection resides in all of us, causing us to pick up a mask to hide our real self. We are guarded in our conversations, always do the right thing, keep all the rules, and outwardly appear to be people of integrity, when just the opposite is the case. We have concluded that being ourselves is not enough, so we pretend to be what other people want or need. We are chameleons who change with the crowd as often as necessary to belong. We don't know who we are, because we have spent our lives reading a room or situation and adapting to our surroundings. We have no sense of identity because our worth is dependent on someone else's determination. We call it flexibility, when in reality it's fickleness. We have learned early on that pleasing others gets attention, approval, affirmation, and significance, so we lay aside our own needs to fit the part. We know how to perform, what to say, how to say it, when to appear, and when to stay away to conform to the need of the moment. We are praised for our selflessness, friendship, and loyalty, when we are really just afraid to disagree or put forward our own opinion. We truly don't know what we personally think, because we have spent our entire life trying to please someone else.

There is a deep sense of loneliness for us when we hide our true selves. Why? The mask is what receives the attention or affirmation. Who we really are doesn't seem to be enough. Instead of recognizing that we have things to offer that others need, we hide and a false self is created. Once the false self starts receiving praise, it seals the persona, because now there is a risk of exposure as a fraud if the real us is revealed. There is nothing wrong with feeling special, but our false self has an attachment to an image that is not true. The problem with the false self is that it works. We forget the vulnerable, small self and take on a bigger, more powerful self that makes us feel valuable, worthwhile, and important. We need to realize that God doesn't love the mask. He loves me. Naked. Me. He doesn't love my appearance, accomplishments, or performance. He loves me. Broken, needy me. And nothing can ever separate me from His love (Rom. 8:39). It is a vulnerable thing to be true to myself, but there is freedom in my honesty.

Mirror Moment

Take a moment and think about when you started wearing your mask. How old were you? What happened for you to decide you needed the mask? Now gather materials to make a mask. It can be as elaborate or simple as you choose. The outside portrays how people see you, and the inside portrays how you see yourself. Be honest with what is really there.

THE WAY THROUGH: OVERVIEW OF SPIRITUAL DISCIPLINES

Spiritual disciplines are like different modes of transportation we use for different trips. Sometimes we choose to walk, ride a bike, ride a motorcycle, or fly in an airplane. Our working definition of spiritual disciplines is a means of grace to make space for God's presence in our lives. In essence, we are saying we are going to remove all distractions occupying our focus so we can give our attention to God. Spiritual disciplines are not a current Christian fad. These disciplines are centuries old and were practiced in the life of Jesus, His disciples, and fellow travelers throughout church history.

Spiritual disciplines are not a checklist to mark off after completion. When we embrace a spiritual discipline and God's presence invades our moment, we linger in that place and allow the Lord to fill us, cleanse us, renew us, encourage us, comfort us, teach us, or correct us. The point of the discipline is to encounter His presence. There is no need to rush or hurry through an assignment. Being with Him is the focus, so when He shows up, we linger there with him.

Spiritual disciplines are not a means of forcing God's hand. For example, some people think that fasting is a way to prove to God how much they love Him, thus forcing Him to do what they want. God will not be held hostage by our immaturity. He doesn't owe us anything just because we go without food. Spiritual disciplines exist to help us make room for the presence of God in our lives so we can figure out what He wants for our lives. Richard Foster wrote,

> When we despair of gaining inner transformation through human powers of will and determination, we are open to a wonderful new realization: inner righteousness is a gift of God to be graciously received. The needed change within us is God's work, not ours. The demand is for an inside job, and only God can work from the inside. We cannot attain or earn this righteousness of the kingdom of God; it is a grace that is given.[13]

---

[13] Richard Foster, *Celebration of Discipline: The Path to Spiritual Growth* (San Francisco: HarperCollins, 1978), 6.

God is the One who changes us; we simply say yes to His promptings and are empowered by His Spirit to be able to change. The spiritual disciplines are the tools by which we make space for God.

Dallas Willard first named the spiritual disciplines of abstinence and spiritual disciplines of engagement, which help us remove barriers that block our connection to God and include practices that nurture our connection to God.[14] In this book, I focus primarily on a few disciplines of abstinence and have taken the liberty to call things spiritual disciplines that are not considered such in the traditional sense. I have done this to introduce new sojourners to the ease of connection with God as we make room for Him in our lives and schedules.[15]

Spiritual Disciplines of Abstinence (Withholding)

The disciplines of abstinence are the means by which we say no to certain things so we can say yes to God. Chastity is the discipline of saying no to sex for a certain period of time, even as a married person, so not to be controlled by it. Celibacy is the permanent choice to live a chaste lifestyle. The discipline of fasting refrains from food or water for a certain length of time for spiritual purposes. Frugality is using little money to do things inexpensively. It differs from sacrifice, in that a person practicing sacrifice has money or wealth and chooses to

---

[14] Dallas Willard, *The Spirit of the Disciplines: Understanding How God Changes Lives* (San Francisco: HarperOne, 1999).
[15] See the written works of the following people to take you deeper into spiritual disciplines and practices: St. Augustine, St. Ignatius, Desert Fathers, Jeanne Guyon, Francois Fenelon, St. Teresa of Avila, Julian of Norwich, Thomas Merton, St. John of the Cross, Henri Nouwen, and Brennan Manning.

give that up to please God. Martyrdom is being willing to die for Christ. Poverty is choosing not to own things. Secrecy is choosing not to let others know the good deeds you do for others. Submission is giving up control. Simplicity is giving up what complicates your life so you can focus more fully on the Lord.

At times, it's obvious what God is speaking to us and at other times, it lacks clarity. His various styles of communication cause us to listen with an intentionality we might otherwise miss. It is a very slow process, but the deeper we go in intimacy, the greater the revelation of unknown entanglements of our heart to other things. The disciplines of solitude, silence, and stillness are disciplines of abstinence which make room for God in very purposeful ways.

Solitude

Solitude is the practice of saying no to noise, busyness, hurry, and community to come to God alone for what you need. I am all for community, but there are times when we try to get from other people what we need to get from God alone. Extroverts who get fed by being with people will have times in their lives when the Lord will ask them to come away with Him and fast from people, noise, busyness, and activity to be alone in His presence. There is something about solitude that allows us to focus on His purpose and His way. It is hard to find places to be alone, but it is vital for our growth. Jesus often practiced solitude. "Very early in the morning, while it was still dark, Jesus got up, left the house and went off to a solitary place, where he prayed" (Mk. 1:35). Getting away from the crowd and all the voices to hear the One Voice puts things in perspective.

Silence

The discipline of silence can be part of the solitude activity. It is a discipline that fasts from noise and words, with the intention of better hearing the voice of God. Vows of silence are a common part of monastic and Franciscan traditions, and with the quickening pace and constant barrage of stimulation from electronics, it is a wise practice to withdraw to the quiet to focus on God. The discipline of silence includes moving to silent places as well as refraining from speaking.

Contemplation or centering prayer often flows out of silence and solitude, but it is a different kind of prayer than found in evangelical traditions. Petitioning God with needs and requests requires explaining ourselves, but centering prayer focuses on God. It almost seems like a pointless exercise, but its goal is to come to God without any agenda, list, or request,

Jesus, you are my healer.

simply to gaze upon His beauty (Ps. 27:4) with a repetitive word or phrase. Phrases can be spoken with the rhythm of one's breathing with two syllables spoken upon inhalation and five syllables spoken upon exhalation. "Jesus" (breathing in), "I trust you alone" (breathing out). Another phrase is, "Abba, I belong to you. Jesus, you are my healer. Father, my hope is in you."

The beauty of this simple exercise is that it requires us to slow down. Even if we come into God's presence frazzled, it helps us calm down as we slowly and deliberately say these phrases. It is important to use meaningful phrases fitting to us as we engage in this new practice.

Repetition of declarative truth is powerful. Time is needed for us to unwind, but done as a repeated practice, it helps us center on the One who is in charge and loves us as we are. We see the power of the angels' repetition whose sole purpose in Revelation 4:8 is to repeat the phrase, "Holy, holy, holy is the Lord God Almighty, who was and is and is to come." This is not a mindless chant; rather, it is an intentional act of worship to humbly adore the Worthy One. Making room in our lives to do the same centers us on Him.

Our tendency is to make our time with God productive by moving quickly from enjoying the presence of the Lord to how God can use us. We must avoid this temptation to come to get to give. We start out coming to God for ourselves, but soon realize that what we are reading or learning would make a good sermon or teaching point for a class we teach. We easily cross the line from personal intimacy to job mode in a very short period of time. Jeanne Guyon wrote,

> Let us say your mind begins to wander. Once you have been deeply touched by the Lord's Spirit and are distracted, be diligent to bring your wandering mind back to the Lord. This is the easiest way in the world to overcome external distractions.[16]

It is normal for our minds to wander, but we must choose to return our attention to the presence of the Lord. God doesn't want something from us. He simply wants us. God desires our wholehearted love and affection. Guyon continues,

> Then, how will you treat suffering? Or, to put it another way, how do you respond to the Lord's working of the cross in your life? You respond this way. As soon as

---

[16] Jeanne Guyon, *Experiencing the Depths of Jesus Christ*, Library of Christian Classics, Volume 2, (Seedsowers Christian Books Publishing House, 1975), 12.

anything comes to you in the form of suffering, at that very moment a natural resistance will well up somewhere inside you. When that moment comes, immediately resign yourself to God. *Accept the matter.* In that moment give yourself up to Him as a sacrifice.[17]

It will not come easily for us to sit silently and do nothing, which is precisely why it is called a discipline.

Stillness

I am adding stillness as a spiritual discipline because many people do not make time for it. They meet God in the shower, in the car, or while cleaning the house. Whichever place you meet the Lord is a great place, *but* there is something powerful about intentionally coming into the presence of the Lord and not multitasking. To sit or lie in one place fully awake and focusing on the Lord opens the door to realize our fear that God might not show up. When we come alone into the presence of the Lord quiet and still, there can be immediate discomfort with the silence and the stillness. Unresolved emotional pain kept at bay while busy now surfaces. Thoughts like, "Is this doing any good? What am I waiting for anyway? What is the point? Am I doing this right? Am I supposed to feel something? What do I think about during this time? How long am I supposed to stay here doing nothing?" And the list goes on and on. These thoughts have to be reined in, which is why the phrases of centering prayer combined with breathing are helpful. A simple prayer like, "Come, Holy Spirit" is a beautiful way to welcome His presence and open our hearts to Him.

---

[17] Guyon, *Experiencing the Depths of Jesus Christ*, 38.

Mirror Moment

Find a comfortable, quiet place and set a timer for eight minutes. Remove all possible distractions, close your eyes, and ask the Holy Spirit to come. You can do the breathing exercise with a phrase that helps you focus on God, or just be still. When the timer goes off, write in your journal what you saw, sensed, heard, or felt during this time of stillness. Don't feel bad if nothing happened. This is where the discipline part comes in. Just keep showing up and God will meet you. Jesus promises, "I will not leave you as orphans; I will come to you" (Jn. 14:18). Waiting is one of the hardest things to do, but it is a normal part of the spiritual journey.

Spiritual Disciplines of Engagement (Connection)

Once we become familiar with solitude, silence, and stillness before God, spiritual disciplines of engagement are added to deepen the connection. Practices such as Bible reading, meditation, Scripture memorization, prayer, and worship help us reinforce biblical truths on which people of faith have relied throughout church history. These practices require an openness to understanding and embracing a life of faith as new ways of living counter our paradigm. Self-reliance falls by the wayside as we move away from being our own god to relying upon another to lead us and care for us. Disciplines of engagement are a more traditional means of connecting with God which many people of faith have experienced in their upbringing, regardless of their religion or church denomination.

Bible reading opens us up to hear from God in a way that pilgrims for centuries have heard the voice of God. Meditation is a conscious focus on small portions of the Bible to ingest their meaning and apply them to your life. The Bible encourages us to "keep this Book of the Law always on your lips; meditate on it day and night, so that you may be careful to do everything written in it. Then you will be prosperous and successful" (Joshua 1:8). Choosing to commit verses to memory provides a weapon against lies by retrieving truth during trying times. Prayer is opening the door to let Jesus in and talk with us providing direction and guidance for our lives. Worship is purposeful devotion to someone to whom we give our time, attention, and money. Participating in these spiritual disciplines of engagement makes room for us to connect with God.

Practice: Reading the Bible

There is plenty of reading material in publication today with differing views on anything we want to know. Reading the Bible is God's perspective and plan for the people on the journey to know who He is, who they are, and how He wants them to live. The Holy Spirit illuminates Scripture to us when we read, so we can understand its meaning and apply it to our lives. There are now phone apps for Bible readings, daily verses, prayer, and devotionals, which you may find helpful. It is also good to have a hard copy Bible so you can see the words in print, underline or highlight areas, and take notes in the margins.

A Bible reading program can be helpful to read different parts of the Bible simultaneously to see the overarching themes of the Bible. One method that is helpful for a themed approach is to daily read one chapter from Psalms, one chapter from Proverbs, one chapter from the Old Testament (starting with Genesis), and one chapter from the New Testament (starting with Matthew). Some people read through the entire Bible every year and use a different translation so there is a freshness to the reading. The goal of Bible reading is to encounter the presence of God, so the length of reading is not as important as connecting with Him.

A system or method of reading is a good way to work your way through the Bible, but in your daily reading, when you experience God, stop right there, linger in His presence, and enjoy what He is saying to you through His word. You can read the verses multiple times, close your eyes, and repeat a phrase that stands out to you. Pray that phrase or verse(s) back to the Lord and tell Him you understand what He is trying to say to you. Depending on the length of time you take to linger, that may be enough for one day. If you have time, you may keep reading until something else stands out to you, and linger in the Lord's presence as previously mentioned. God wants you to understand what He's saying to you. Make room for Him and give time to reading His words.

DISCUSSION QUESTIONS

1. What is your family's background of spirituality, and where are you on the journey?

2. Are the people, places, and habits in your life helping or hindering your relationship with God? Explain. Share what you wrote in this Mirror Moment.

3. What do you think or feel when you read that God desires to have relationship with you?

4. Which type(s) of people on the journey are you: (theoretician, diagnostician, observer, practitioner? Explain.

5. How does the fear of rejection play a role in your life?

6. In what way(s) do your feelings of worth affect your relationships?

7. Share with your group the mask you made during your mirror moment. Start with the outside, then move to the inside. It may be helpful for you to share the one thing you hope no one ever finds out about you, because this is the place where your feelings of worth are hooked. Speaking the truth releases that hold on you and allows the grace and love of God through others to be extended to you.

Chapter 3.

BELONGING: A PLACE WHERE I AM ACCEPTED AS I AM

At a deep psychological level, convincing young people that they will get the respect, admiration, love that they are looking for through consumerism is a manipulation of a deep human instinct to want to belong.[18]
—HELENA NORBERG-HODGE

Years ago, when I attended church conferences, I would feel a pit in my stomach. There was an unspoken prevailing attitude that women were allowed to attend, but not necessarily invited to contribute. We knew our place as women, needed to stay in our lane, and needed to keep our mouths shut. Needless to say, that is not a good feeling. It's better today, but there are

---

[18] Helena Norberg-Hodge, interviewed by Jemima Roberts, a columnist from The Ecologist on March 2, 2011, http://www.theecologist.org/green_green_living/Q_and_A/794238/qa_helena_norberghodge.html.

still issues that need to be addressed. Many church denominations and even parachurch organizations state that they are for women in ministry. In theory and even in theology that may be true, but their practice often lags far behind. This attitude affects true fellowship and withholds one part of the body from operating at full capacity. There is an obvious ceiling and such attitudes cause women to die a little bit inside, refusing to seek to attain their full potential. Growing and developing appears ambitious and somehow takes away from a man leading. How does one person becoming all that God created her to be impinge on someone else's growth or leadership? It doesn't. Sons *and daughters* belong together in the kingdom to live and work side by side. I love the line from the worship song that says, "In my Father's house, there's a place for me." There is room for everyone in the kingdom of God to walk in the fullness of their gifts and calling.

Belonging is more felt that stated. Telling people they belong is one thing, but making room for them speaks much louder than words. An invitation to a party, conversation, committee, or neighborhood doesn't mean acceptance. True belonging means love and acceptance *as you are* to experience community, accountability, fellowship, and healing.

STRONG BODY

The apostle Paul used an example of belonging in I Corinthians 12:15–20 when he wrote about having one body with many parts. It is impossible for the body to be considered as separate parts, because no part can exist on its own. An eye, ear, or head by itself will not live. Each needs the connection with the whole to function. Individual parts of the body may not be able to operate at full capacity, causing a deficiency or disability, but the sum of all parts makes up the whole. The Corinthians passage continues with verses 21–26.

> The eye cannot say to the hand, "I don't need you!" And the head saying to the feet, "I don't need you!" On the contrary, those parts of the body that seem to be weaker are indispensable and the parts that we think are less honorable we treat with special honor... But God has put the body together, giving greater honor to the parts that lacked it, so that there should be no division in the body, but that its parts should have equal concern for each other. If one part suffers, every part suffers with it; if one part is honored, every part rejoices with it.

The emphasis is on the fact that God is the One who has put the body together. Every part is needed for the body to be healthy and function properly. Belonging deepens the connection and sends the message that each individual part matters and contributes to the whole.

FOUR SPACES OF BELONGING

Have you ever felt like you didn't belong? Belonging is a basic human need, intended to first be experienced in the relationship of family. Community is a place where a person is deeply loved, wanted, needed, and appreciated. There is no need to pretend or seek to earn approval in community, because acceptance is a given. Several levels of belonging within community deepen relationships and create intimacy.

Anthropologist Edward T. Hall studied spatial distances to see how people communicate within cultures. These four spaces of belonging include public, social, personal, and intimate. The commonalities of all four spaces include connection, participation, commitment, and significance.[19]

In public belonging spaces, people connect through an outside influence, such as a professional sports team. People wear official garb, buy special broadcast viewing privileges, and stay up too late or get up extra early just to see the results of the game. Another example of public belonging is a political party. People from various regions of the country who are very different in every area of their lives are united in supporting the same candidate. The political party is the outside influence that joins these people.

Social belonging occurs when people share snapshots of what it would be like to be in personal space together. The phrases "first impression" and "put your best foot forward" refer to this spatial belonging. Social belonging is important because it provides the space for "neighbor" relationships. A neighbor is someone you know well enough to ask for small favors. Such a relationship provides a space for those who would like to develop a deeper relationship. In social space, information is provided that helps others decide if connection is possible.

Personal belonging relationships share private experiences, feelings, and thoughts. These relationships are deeper than casual acquaintances, and yet knowing the information doesn't cause discomfort. People who connect in these spaces are close friends.

Intimate belonging relationships go even deeper, and people know the naked truth about each other and are not

---

[19] Edward T. Hall, *The Hidden Dimension* (New York: Anchor Books Doubleday, 1966).

ashamed. There is deep vulnerability in such relationships, with very few people sharing in this capacity. Belonging is very important for people to be healthy members of society. Healthy community is achieved when we hold harmonious connections within all four spaces.

Mirror Moment

Take a moment and reflect on the close relationships in your life.

List the people who share your personal belonging relationships.

List the people who share your intimate belonging relationships. To what depth do you share with these people? Do they know everything about you, or are you still guarded in some areas of your heart? Is there anyone in your life with whom you are emotionally and spiritually intimate?

OBSTACLE: SHAME

If you have ever done something you weren't proud of, then you know that shame is the accomplice of a bad choice. It is an obstacle to belonging because it categorically separates and isolates like nothing else. Why do we allow shame to define us? Shame is an overwhelming sense of exclusive defectiveness that is accompanied by the belief that it is impossible to change. It carries both the feeling and belief that something is innately wrong with me; therefore, I will never quite belong. I am in attendance, part of the group, and even well liked, but always present is the underlying sense of being different. Difference of this kind is not the unique, special, one of a kind, or no one else in the world like you wonderful different.

This difference means there is something about me that is deficient, lacking, or unacceptable. In short, *I* am bad. Not what I did is bad, rather I am bad. Shame becomes the barrier to self-acceptance. It blocks the needed engagement with others that would help us feel love and belonging.

Shame leads to self-rejection and is often accompanied by a feeling of invisibility, as if living in a dream, with no one able to see or hear you. Present, but disconnected. The evil intention behind shame is to dismantle your God-given identity and destroy you as an individual. If self is rejected, community connections will be fleeting and superficial, because love cannot be given or received. Shame breeds self-rejection.

Figure 1 shows the Shame Cycle. Shame starts with a trigger. It can take place as early as fifteen to eighteen months by the response to something as small as a look, a sigh, a frown, or a gesture. Toddlers cannot even speak at this age, yet these nonverbal cues carry the undeniable felt message of disapproval.[20] Similar triggers throughout our lives activate the shame cycle, causing feelings of inferiority. The emotion then moves to judgment, both from others and self. Statements like, "There you go again, idiot," "You're so stupid." "You never get it right, do you?" can start the cycle. Comments of correction, redirection, and even affirmation can equally initiate the cycle: "Don't worry about it. I'll finish up here." "You go to the party. I'll stay home with the kids." "Didn't so and so do a great job on her report?" Shame is an equal opportunity destroyer that sneaks up at any place at any time to upset a person's emotional equilibrium. Self-judgment may be more

---

[20] For an extensive study of shame, see Michael Lewis, *Shame: The Exposed Self* (New York: The Free Press, 1995).

brutal than other people's words as familiar self-talk tapes play a continuous loop of reproach, beratement, and self-hatred.

The third part of the cycle consists of hiding. The person immediately withdraws to seek cover from the disapproval of others. Emotional withdrawal is certain and is often accompanied by physical withdrawal if possible. Examples of physical hiding caused by shame include avoiding social gatherings, excusing oneself to go to the bathroom in the middle of a conversation, asking for a minute to regroup, changing the subject, or abruptly disengaging in a discussion. Hiding of this sort only lasts long enough to pull it together emotionally before being physically able to leave the room.

Hiding moves into the fourth phase of the cycle called disconnection. In this phase, a person disconnects from self and others by participating in distractive behaviors that dull the pain of shame. Whether or not the engagement is periodic or frequent, the purpose of the behavior is to escape from the pervasive feelings of disapproval, worthlessness, and inferiority. Such disconnection leads to the final phase of the cycle, called reinforced isolation, whereby a person chooses to be alone rather than pursue relationship. The disparaging emotional drain that shame inflicts on a person's mind and heart crushes the hope of change.

Have you let shame be your guide? Shame is subtle and secretive in its search for entrance into our lives. It silently lives in the shadows of our soul, waiting for the opportune time to expose and humiliate us. In the blink of an eye, we are in the middle of a shame cycle, reeling from its sudden and impactful pounce. Movement through this cycle

> Shame is subtle and secretive in its search for entrance into our lives.

can happen in a matter of seconds, concurrently persisting with guilt over wasted time, wasted money, or bingeing on pointless activities. Perpetuation of the cycle continues until broken by new thought patterns.

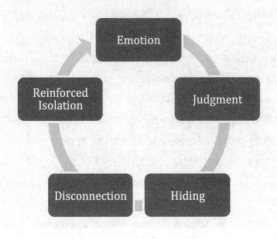

Figure 1: Shame Cycle

Figure 2 shows the Grace Cycle and the needed elements of change for healthy thinking. The first phase of this cycle, like the Shame Cycle, also starts with emotion, but is followed by acceptance rather than judgment. Other people's jeering remarks or hurtful comments continue as always, but now are not received unfavorably. The grid or filter of shame through which a person has viewed the world has been removed and with that removal comes the ability to love others in all their flawed glory. Grace is extended to others for their careless-ness. Negative self-talk is replaced with truthful statements like, "I am a beloved child of the King" and "My security is established by receiving the love of the Father." Grace breeds self-acceptance.

This level of acceptance leads to the third phase of the grace cycle, called living in the light. In this phase, the person is transparent and has no need to hide. Mistakes are seen as a normal part of life in which lessons can be learned. There is no fear of taking risks because even failure is seen as opportunity for growth.

There is no fear of taking risks because even failure is seen as opportunity for growth.

While in the fourth phase of the grace cycle, an individual keeps a mental and physical connection with others. The choice to stay in the present moment allows the individual to feel the pain and grieve the losses that accompany the pain. Connection with one's own thoughts and feelings then allows the individual to move to the final stage of a supportive community to work through the losses in order to release them, receive healing, and live in truth.

Figure 2: Grace Cycle

One of the beautiful things about a supportive community is the presence of others to hold us accountable for our actions. Rather than running wild, doing our own thing, and not considering anyone else, accountability provides a voice of reason. It is a safety feature to keep us from running amuck. Motivations are kept in check, ambition is acknowledged, and reasons for certain mindsets, behaviors, and actions are explained to another person to reveal blind spots we would not see otherwise.

SUPPORTIVE COMMUNITY

We need community. The book of Hebrews exhorts the reader, "Let us draw near to God, let us hold unswervingly to the hope we profess, let us spur one another on toward love and good deeds, encourage one another and let us not give up meeting together" (10:22–25). It appears from this passage that meeting together in community is where we can gain strength to be able to do these things. Daily interactions with others who know us and love us challenge us to face inconsistencies in our lives and change our thinking patterns, attitudes, and behaviors. *The Message* version of Ephesians 4:4 states, "You were all called to travel on the same road and in the same direction, so stay together, both outwardly and inwardly." Such togetherness provides the necessary connection and accountability in actions and thoughts to keep us emotionally and spiritually healthy.

It can work the other way as well. A community that does not know God encourages each other, spurs each other, and holds onto hope, but it is a self-centered attempt to feel better with other people who do not want to draw near to God. There is not really any standard to live by other than the one in your own head. It is an attitude whereby you will live as you want and do as you please, with no accountability. A community that draws near to God does not live by its own standard; rather, it lives by the standard of God according to the Word of God. There is a surrendering to someone outside of self and greater than self. Surrender is not a popular concept. It is considered weakness to voluntarily give up one's will to the will of another. What is not realized is that in the surrendering comes a security established by love. There is deep connection that occurs between the two parties because a new way has opened opportunity for intimacy. In Christianity, this new way is through faith in Jesus Christ. His sacrifice of love opened the way for people to be able to draw near to God.

Fellowship is definitely a church word coming from passages in the New Testament that describe strong community. People need deep connection that goes beyond shallow pleasantries and small talk and moves to deep connection and understanding. True fellowship welcomes the depth of relationship and the accountability that accompanies it. Supportive community provides the possibility of healing. It is in community where wounding occurs, but it is also in community where healing occurs—not in isolation. It takes courage to continue to enter into relationships because there is always the potential for pain, misunderstanding, and loss. Perseverance is needed to continue to seek healing and trust others.

THE WAY THROUGH: DISCIPLINE OF COMMUNITY

Conflict is not an excuse to avoid community. As we live together in community and our lives touch each other, sooner or later, differences arise and cause conflict. It is during these times that what we are truly like inside spills out and our character is revealed. In the midst of daily living, our character is developed as problems are worked through in order to keep the relationship. It is very easy in a cyber world to simply cut off relationship by refusing to text someone, refusing to make phone calls, blocking that person on all social media, and removing a person from your instant message contacts. True community chooses to keep communicating, no matter how awkward the situation, in order to resolve misunderstandings and preserve the relationship.

SAFE PLACE

Community provides a safe place for others to reveal what is going on inside them. Henri Nouwen wrote, "The man who can articulate the movements of his inner life need no longer be a victim of himself, but is able slowly and consistently to remove the obstacles that prevent the Spirit from entering."[21] Community provides opportunity for a person to identify and remove obstacles that are impeding personal relationship with Jesus. Community is honest and doesn't just tell us what we want to hear. Community can be as small or as large as we are comfortable, and it involves giving other people permission to speak into our lives.

Living life together in community means intentionality. It involves fun and laughter as well as dealing with inner heart and soul issues that are dark and painful. Love and acceptance provide a place for us to be honest with ourselves and others

---

[21] Henri Nouwen, *The Wounded Healer: Ministry in Contemporary Society* (Dobbs Ferry: Doubleday, 1972), 38.

as to what is really going on under the surface. Only by openly exposing those areas to another does true community occur. It is a safe place to be able to share hopes, dreams, failures, problems, and fears and welcome others to speak into that area of our life to offer hope and healing. Other perspectives are important to identify blind spots and areas of strength that we cannot see on our own. A community speaks truth to us to help us see what God sees. At times, self-awareness is painful and cannot be accomplished without others to hold the mirror. Oftentimes what is seen is better than what a person internally believes, but would have never been identified without the help of others. Community is a gift from God to speak His words of love, affirmation, significance, and acceptance as well as instruction, correction, rebuke, and reprimand. First John 3:16 reads, "This is how we know what love is: Jesus Christ laid down his life for us. And we ought to lay down our lives for our brothers and sisters."

TRUE FRIENDSHIP IN COMMUNITY

Who is in your community that you trust? I have three close friends who are part of my community. We try to meet weekly to talk about everything and anything that is bothering us and needs to be processed. Talking to the point of self-discovery is all part of what we call processing. Sometimes the consistency of our meeting times wanes due to work schedules and family needs, but there is deep connection, love, and trust among us that is very dear to each of us. It is safe to tell it like it is and not have to filter anything. Attentive friends with us in our pain, frustration, indecision, anger, restlessness, joy, passion, and dreaming are a precious gift. Being together means offering time and space for the one talking to put into words all that is felt. Moments of silence are shared together as the talker searches for words to articulate what is causing her dissonance. The silence enables the talker to keep going as more vulnerable thoughts surface. A timely clarifying or reflective question often helps cut through the emotion to help her pinpoint the real issue.

Once she is able to identify exactly what is bothering her, she can then honestly evaluate her part in it. Oftentimes the underlying issue is fear—more specifically a fear of the unknown or fear of the future. "What if" scenarios bombard her mind, and she realizes she has been managing her fear through control. As she looks back, she sees that she has been nitpicking at her husband and children because they are not cooperating with this tactic. Control doesn't build relationships, nor does it foster trust. Instead, forcing control causes others' resistance and tension, which only escalates her efforts. An angry blowup usually occurs and hopefully causes her to withdraw and look within instead of blaming everyone else for their lack of cooperation.

Tears are common during these times as unmet expectations arise to accompany her fear. There is no pressure from the listeners to fix anything. Advice or opinions are not given unless requested by the talker. This enables the listener to have a deeper level of attentiveness. Space enables the talker to keep talking without concern for interruption or losing her train of thought. Being together becomes a safe place for her to express what is really going on with support, honesty, and love in return.

TELL IT LIKE IT IS

The church is called to be the community of truth who brings things into the light and lives transparently. In the Greek, the word for truth is *aletheia*, meaning "not concealed." No hiding. No cover-up. There is something very powerful about bringing to light the dark secrets of your life where no one has been allowed to enter. Psalm 32:3 reads, "When I kept silent, my bones wasted away through my groaning all day long... Then I acknowledged my sin to you and did not cover up my iniquity. I said, 'I will confess my transgression to the Lord.' And you forgave the guilt of my sin." Bringing our secrets into the light disarms their hold on our lives. Left in our minds, secrets grow as we add assumptions and paranoia to the mix. We are determined that everyone knows what we are trying to hide and we drive ourselves crazy with our inner self-talk. When we bring our secrets into the light, we see them for what they really are. We face them directly and can solve them piece by piece. Our willingness to come into the light also invites the perspective of our safe community to speak into our lives and help us.

Gathering together in groups for spiritual development is becoming more popular in many churches today, but has been happening throughout church history. The Pietist movement was a movement of spiritual renewal that reacted against the immoral character of clergy who had a job as clergy with no evident life of Christ. Philipp Jakob Spener started this movement after his book in 1675, *Pia Desideria* (Pious Wishes), popularized his ideas. This movement was for people in the church who were concerned about their own salvation and wanted a place to gather in groups for encouragement. His aim was not to separate the church, but to gather it together for personal conversion with holiness of life, close fellowship in small groups, and the responsibility for missionary outreach.

The Moravians and the early Methodists formed their followers into small groups and used accountability questions to draw out honesty by asking, "How are things with your soul?" In 1722, some of the Moravian Hussites came under persecution and sought freedom in Saxony, Germany, where Count Nikolaus von Zinzendorf took them in and established a community devoted to prayer, praise, and Bible study. The summer of 1727 was considered the golden summer when revival came to twenty-four men and women who made a covenant to spend one hour a day in prayer, and for the next one hundred years, there was never a stoppage in prayer. Much spiritual growth can happen in community.

In order for us to be free, we must intentionally live in the light. Our community doesn't allow us to hide and withdraw. They encourage, support, and challenge us to stay in the present moment to face the difficult things in our lives and are right there with us in the process.

PRACTICE: ASKING FOR HELP

One of the best ways to fight shame is to ask others for help. By reaching out to others, we come out of hiding, and isolation is broken by connecting with others. The more we do it, the more comfortable it becomes to ask. Make a conscious effort to ask for help at least once a day for a week. By doing so, we will find that people are genuinely agreeable to help in any way they can, and we may meet a new person who fits our safe place community.

DISCUSSION QUESTIONS

1. Describe your safe place community. On a scale of one to ten, with one being superficial and ten being deep, what is the level of depth in this community?

2. Do you view vulnerability as a strength or weakness? Why?

3. Explain which of Edward Hall's four spaces is the most difficult for you to make connection with others.

4. How does shame hold you back from relationships?

5. How has your community provided both wounding and healing?

6. Describe the degree of ease you have in asking for help.

Chapter 4.

BROKENNESS: THE AREA OF MY LIFE I HOPE NO ONE EVER FINDS OUT ABOUT ME

Where there is great anxiety, people-pleasing, anger, phobias, and the drive to control, there is usually a false belief and deep wounding. Brokenness traps us into destructive patterns, which eventually destroys much of what is good in our lives.[22]
—TERRY WARDLE

If you have ever felt broken or anxious, you know it can be hard to cover it up. In Matthew 5:3, when Jesus started his Sermon on the Mount, the first thing he declared was, "Blessed are the poor in spirit, for theirs is the kingdom of heaven." Another term for "poor in spirit" is broken. Those who are broken tend

---

[22] Terry Wardle, *Outrageous Love, Transforming Power: How the Holy Spirit Shapes You into the Likeness of Christ* (Leafwood Publishers, 2004), 99.

not to wear a mask, because there is no need to hide. They know they are broken and are willing and open to receive any and all help to mend their brokenness.

There were two groups of people listening to Jesus that day. One group was the religious leaders who had it all together and lacked nothing. They were not broken or poor in spirit. The other group had nothing to offer God or anyone else. They were completely and utterly broken before God; however, they were the ones Jesus said would receive His kingdom. Jesus wanted people to know that they could come to God as they are and He would receive them. There was no need to clean up first and try to look presentable. Broken people know they need help and are welcome in the kingdom.

> Broken people know they need help and are welcome in the kingdom.

In American culture, it is considered great weakness to admit lack. In 1984, the Gillette Company launched a new series of TV commercials for its Dry Idea antiperspirant slogan "never let 'em see you sweat." The commercials included a famous fashion designer, the head coach of the Denver Broncos, an actress, and a comedian. Each person gave three "nevers" in their particular script, but each one ended with the phrase "never let 'em see you sweat." The message was that no matter how difficult things got, never show weakness. For Americans, it is a normal thing to portray strength; however, vulnerability is considered a big no-no. We are "the land of the free and the home of the brave," not the home of the scared, weak, vulnerable, and broken. The apostle Paul wrote in I Corinthians 1:27–29,

But God chose the foolish things of the world to shame the wise; God chose the weak things of the world to shame the strong. God chose the lowly things of this world and the despised things—and the things that are not—to nullify the things that are, so that no one may boast before him.

Recognizing our weakness and receiving help from someone greater than ourselves is considered a strength in the kingdom of God.

JESUS' BROKENNESS

We often forget that Jesus came for the broken. He came to experience this life and see how it felt to be broken. Isaiah 53:3 aptly described Jesus' brokenness. "He was despised and rejected by mankind, a man of suffering and familiar with pain. Like one from whom people hide their faces he was despised and we held him in low esteem." Despised, rejected, suffered, pain, pierced, crushed, oppressed, and afflicted are all descriptors of brokenness. Verse 5 continues, "But he was pierced for our transgressions, he was crushed for our iniquities; the punishment that brought us peace was on him and by his wounds we are healed." Jesus was broken so those who looked to him could live. Jesus chose death so we could experience life—a simple exchange for those who believe. Our God knows and understands brokenness. By choosing Him, our brokenness is restored with healing and wholeness.

Psalm 51 gives us a look into David's prayer life as he poured out his heart to God after the prophet Nathan called out his sin of committing adultery with Bathsheba. Verse 17 reads, "The sacrifices of God are a broken spirit; a broken and contrite heart, you will not despise." The Hebrew word here for broken is *shabar,* meaning "crippled, maimed, wrecked, and crushed." This is what happened to Jesus on his way to the cross. David is saying God will not despise a spirit or heart in this condition because Jesus was despised on our behalf so our worth could be restored. Man despises brokenness, but God never will.

WE ARE ALL BROKEN

In the spring of 1993, our children were ages five, three, and one when I became pregnant with our fourth child. My husband and I were busy with ministry, having planted a church in Northern California only a few years before, and I was overwhelmed with motherhood, since both of our families lived on the East Coast. Anger toward the children began to come out in disproportionate ways, and I didn't know what to do. If I was with them in the grocery store and they began to whine, I would take them into the bathroom and spank them really hard. If they spilled their drink during a meal, I would go into a rage. To add more pressure to the situation, I homeschooled the oldest two children and would scream at them when they got distracted or didn't understand what I was trying to teach them. I was a hot mess and needed help. The worst part was, I didn't dare to reveal how bad it was.

One day, I finally got up enough courage to tell my husband I needed help, and he brushed it off that I had probably just had a bad day. I firmly told him that was not the case. I had purposely controlled myself when he was around, so I needed him to understand how bad things were. I told him I wanted to meet with our pastor, because he had shared in his sermons about his anger issues. I believed he would understand and hopefully be able to help me.

The next day in church while our pastor was preaching, a woman in the back began a long, loud wail. The ushers went to help her out of the room when the pastor stopped his sermon and told them to leave her alone and turn up his microphone. He relayed that she was finally feeling much unresolved pain and needed to let it out. He continued to preach and another woman on the other side of the room also let out a long, loud wail. I was sitting beside my husband in the front row, and as he began to shift in his seat, I knew he was uncomfortable with what was happening in the room. Little did he know, that any minute I was going to be one of those wailing women.

As the pastor described living from the false self, he simply said, "It's okay not to be okay." The moment I heard that statement, I felt a deep resonance in my gut and a wave of emotion begin to rise in me. I had grown up in a Christian home and attended church my entire life. I knew how to behave in church. That day, those words gave me permission to be honest. I was not okay and I knew it, but I had learned to do the right thing at the right time in the right place and therefore, things would be all right. My rightness was all wrong! I held it together until the altar call and then knelt on the floor in front of my seat and cried and cried and cried. Hiding the terrible secret of my raging anger was over and I was relieved. My brokenness was now out in the open.

I began to meet weekly with the pastor and his wife for prayer and counseling to begin the journey of establishing new habits and patterns of thinking, extending and receiving forgiveness, and identifying the fear and hurt underneath the anger. The first step to my freedom was bringing my brokenness into the light. I released the guilt of my actions and the shame I carried that I was disqualified for ministry because of my sin and brokenness. Have you ever felt like you had to fix yourself before you could come to God and receive the healing you knew you needed? The reality of it is that our sin and brokenness qualify us to receive the grace and mercy of Jesus as our savior and healer.

I believed Psalm 34:18: "The Lord is close to the brokenhearted and saves those who are crushed in spirit." I was devastated that I was hurting my children and continuing the cycle of abuse that could be traced back for generations in my family. I clung to Psalm 147:3: "He heals the brokenhearted and binds up their wounds." I was in bondage to anger. I knew that Jesus was my only hope. If Jesus came to "bind up the brokenhearted, to proclaim freedom for the captives and release from darkness for the prisoners" (Is. 61:1), then I had to let Him into this dark place of my brokenness. That decision changed everything. When I admitted my need and welcomed Him into that area of my life, I experienced His tenderness and healing love.

Mirror Moment

Reflect for a moment on the place of your brokenness. What is the one thing you hope no one finds out about you? That is probably the place of your brokenness. Write out the story of your brokenness in your journal, describing the feelings that surround it. Allow the Lord to comfort you in the midst of this exercise. Holding the secret is what gives it power in your life to harass and torment you. "When I remained silent, my bones wasted away through my groaning all day long" (Ps. 32:3).

Find a safe person with whom you can share this journal entry who can direct you to the help you need to begin the healing process.

TWO BROTHERS' BROKENNESS

In Luke 15, we read the story of two brothers. The youngest brother asked for his inheritance so he could go off on his own and live as he pleased. In Jewish culture, a son's request for his inheritance was a sign of great disrespect to the father, indicating that the son cared nothing for relationship with his father, but only wanted his money. The father granted this son's request and gave him his share of the property. After he spent all he had, there was a severe famine in the whole country, so the son got a job feeding pigs. He was starving and desperate enough to eat the pods fed to the pigs. In the midst of his utter state of brokenness, the young man decided to return home and ask his father if he could become a hired servant. "But while he was still a long way off, his father saw him and was filled with compassion for him; he ran to his son, threw his arms around him and kissed him" (Lk 15:20). The father ignored the son's confession of sin against heaven and him and called for a feast to celebrate the return of his son.

His full acceptance of his son was unheard of in that culture. The elders of the town daily sat at the city gates. If they had seen the son before the father, they would have turned him away and refused to let him enter, because of his previous disrespect to his father by asking for his inheritance and bringing shame to the family name. The father knew that would be the case, so every day he scanned the horizon for any sign of his son. Finally, the day came when the father saw him in the distance, ran to him, embraced him, and called for a feast, inviting the entire village to attend. By the father's gracious act of forgiveness toward his son, he was making a statement to the village that his son was fully accepted and should be treated with full rights and privileges as his son.

Such a generous demonstration of love and grace was unprecedented in that culture.

Meanwhile, the older brother was not as pleased about the news of the party. He was angry and refused to attend, even after his father's pleading. His response reveals his brokenness.

> "Look! All these years I've been slaving for you and never disobeyed your orders. Yet you never gave me even a young goat so I could celebrate with my friends. But when this son of yours who has squandered your property with prostitutes comes home, you kill the fattened calf for him!" (Lk. 15:29)

Such a strong, negative, and emotional response of the older son indicated that he had been acting out of duty, interpreting all interaction with his father as obligation. He was hurt and perhaps felt overlooked as the father grieved the loss of the younger son. The father was shocked that his oldest son felt that way and said, "You are always with me and everything I have is yours." This son was unable to receive the love of the father and the rights and privileges that came with the relationship. His brokenness was in his self-righteous attitude and intentional "perfect" behavior. The eldest son was prodigal while living in the father's house.

Brokenness has many facets. Whether a person blatantly rebels outwardly like the younger brother or inwardly seethes from jealousy like the older brother, both are signs of brokenness that need a healing touch. Both sons rebelled against the father. Both sons rejected and abandoned the father. Both sons reacted in ways that revealed their brokenness. Outward signs of brokenness might include rage, abuse, and addictions to alcohol, drugs, sex, or food; but a self-righteous attitude, perfectionism, pride, and judgment of others are just as strong indicators of brokenness that are veiled with morality and good behavior.

The lepers, blind, lame, deaf, demonized, and prostitutes all ran to Jesus to receive love and mercy. The Pharisees and other religious leaders ran *from* Jesus because they refused to accept their brokenness. The younger son ran from the Father and returned to receive grace. The older son was always with the Father, but refused to have a love relationship with Him. In the kingdom of God, there is no limit to God's grace. He will give as much grace as needed. He simply wants us to admit our brokenness and come to Him. Cynthia Pearl Maus described the rise from brokenness from the story of the sinful woman in Luke 7.

> The creative power of Jesus' love called the repentant woman to regard herself as he did, to see in herself the possibilities that he saw in her. The place that this transformed woman occupies in Christian thought is not due to her strange, deep love for Jesus, but rather to what was wrought in her by Christ's love for her. It was Christ's love for her that delivered her from her past [brokenness] and made her what she became. The central truth for which her life has come to stand is that it is possible to be delivered, through love, from the lowest depths to the shining heights where God dwelleth.[23]

The power of love, if we choose to accept it, can be transformational in our lives. Jesus is the only one who sees our

---

[23] Cynthia Pearl Maus, *Christ and the Fine Arts: An Anthology of Pictures, Poetry, Music and Stories Centering in the Life of Christ* (New York: Harper & Brothers, 1938).

utter brokenness and chooses to love us unconditionally. It is this kind of love that gives us hope and the ability to change. This truly is a blessing to the broken.

OBSTACLE: ANGER

Every single one of us is going to feel angry at some time in our lives. Where that anger is directed and why is the starting point of beginning to better understand it. Anger is a strong feeling of displeasure and antagonism aroused by a sense of injury or wrong.[24] Anger develops as "a natural response of the failure of others to meet one's needs for love, praise, acceptance, and justice."[25]

Healthy anger can act as a powerful force for producing change in our lives at every level. It can be a gift that signals that things are not okay. Many people don't think they have a problem with anger, but are sarcastic, passive-aggressive, numb, or apathetic. Each of these expressions is an indication of indirect anger. The word *sarcasm* means "tearing of flesh." It is intended to cut a person, but is covered with a façade of joking. Passive-aggressive people say one thing to our face, then stab us in the back when we turn away. They smile at us and pretend everything is fine, then say things to others, often acting as a victim, to get other people to confront us or speak for them, because they *can't* approach us. This type of manipulation is calculated and driven by anger.

---

[24] Solomon Schimmel (1979) Anger and Its Control in Graeco-Roman and Modern Psychology. *Psychiatry* 42: 320–337.
[25] Robert D. Enright and Joanna North, eds. *Exploring Forgiveness.* Madison, WI, USA: University of Wisconsin Press, 1998. ProQuest ebrary.

People who feel numb have shut down emotionally to survive. Long-term chaotic or abusive situations cause them to close off emotionally to cope. They no longer feel joy or pain. They live in a constant state of numbness and their anger has become frozen. Apathy is a sign that passion and hope are gone. Not caring is the only way a hurting person endures the pain. Apathy is a logical conclusion to an emotional issue. Rather than caring and feeling continual hurt, fear, or power-lessness, a person chooses not to care so they can function in everyday life.

THREE TYPES OF ANGER

Of which type of anger do you most commonly struggle? There are three types of anger mentioned in the New Testament. The first type includes a stewing or festering that brews just below the surface and doesn't come out. The Greek word for this type of anger is *parogizo*, used in Ephesians 6:4, exhorting fathers not to provoke their children to anger. The second type of anger occurs when something important to you is threatened or damaged, gradually building within you. The Greek word is *orgizo*, used in Ephesians 4:26: "Be angry (orgizo), but do not sin; do not let the sun go down on your anger (parogizo) and give no opportunity to the devil." Paul is saying to feel the anger, but don't sin by refusing to deal with the festering anger below the surface which gives the devil a place in your life. The third type of anger is the kind I exhibited with my children. The Greek word is *thymos*, or rage, referred to in Galatians 5:20 as "outbursts of anger" or "fits of rage." This kind of anger passionately erupts, then cools down quickly.

WHAT IS UNDER THE ANGER?

It is very difficult and takes time to break old thought patterns and behaviors. Let's explore six emotional causes under anger. Anger is what presents itself to others, but the primary emotion is underneath the anger. The understanding of these six causes identifies the real issue. The first is fear. Fear can be a strong emotion, causing you to feel weak, vulnerable, and powerless, so you rise up in anger to push people away to regain a sense of control. The rush of adrenaline that accompanies anger makes you feel strong and hides the hidden terror.

The second underlying emotional cause is invalidation of your opinion and feelings. Everyone wants to be heard, whether in a business meeting or at the dinner table. Your opinion is simply your viewpoint on a topic. To criticize your viewpoint or worse yet, ignore you completely, can cause anger. This is often seen in autocratic homes where one parent is always right and children aren't allowed to have different opinions.

The third underlying emotional cause arises when your way is blocked. It is the attitude from which road rage stems—"Get out of my way!" Whether a person's car is cut off on the freeway, or the budget is cut dissolving the business plan, or a two-year-old is told no, anger results. It is probably the most volatile of all the underlying causes, because it erupts spontaneously.

The fourth underlying cause for anger is hurt. When a person is hurt, the offense is either turned inward, leading to despair or depression, or turned outward, leading to anger and bitterness. When turned inward, you seek to contain the anger by taking it out on yourself, and self-rejection and self-hatred results. Turning the hurt outward can lead to blame and seeking revenge toward the person who hurt you. The healthy response to hurt is to feel the sadness, loss, and pain of the wounding.

The fifth underlying cause for anger is attacking your personhood. Name-calling, which is inappropriate comments about your gender, ethnicity, sexuality, or beliefs fits this category. Oftentimes, these comments are made sarcastically or with a joking tone to get a laugh. Outwardly, people might smile or play along, but inwardly the very core of your being has been touched and it hurts.

The final underlying cause for anger is unmet expectations. The angry person flies off the handle because of an unfulfilled expectation that is never spoken to the person receiving the anger. The angry person assumes the expectation is obvious, so he or she doesn't need to communicate it directly. It should just be known. This happens in any relationship with assumptions and poor communication. (Wait, all of us do this at times. Yes, we do.)

Fights cause anger that leave a wake of pain. The next time anger wells up, pause for a moment and sift through these six areas to identify its underlying cause. Clear communication can avoid many arguments and disagreements in our relationships.

HOW DO I GET RID OF MY ANGER?

No one wants to spend all of their time overwhelmed by anger. While you can't rid yourself of anger, because it is an emotion, you can learn to appropriately deal with the real issue under the anger so it doesn't fester or spew in unhealthy ways to hurt people around you.

Here are five ways to self-check your anger level for your personal soul care: 1) Acknowledge the way in which anger generally surfaces—aggression, passive-aggressiveness, sarcasm, numbness, apathy, depression, or rage. Once the form is recognized. 2) Identify the underlying issue as the source—fear, invalidation of your opinion, get out of my way, hurt, attacking my personhood, or unmet expectations. 3) Ask for help. Speaking out your pain to a close friend, spouse, or counselor disarms its power in your mind. 4) Grieve the loss accompanying the pain to process all the feelings surrounding the incident. 5) Choose to forgive the offender.

Forgiveness does not always mean reconciliation for those who have hurt you and may not ever involve a conversation with the other person. Rather, forgiveness eliminates bitterness from forming in your heart to torment you and cut off intimacy with God and those you love. Satan is a roaring lion looking for someone to devour. Do not allow unhealthy anger to be the entry point of your destruction. You can be free from anger's grip. Go beneath it and diffuse it.

THE WAY THROUGH: DISCIPLINE OF FORGIVENESS

Are you ready for a path to freedom? The way through anger at others is forgiving them by choosing to release your own heart from the burden of offense. Offense can either be self-inflicted or caused by others, but letting go of it is what brings freedom to you. There is a lie attached to unforgiveness that by holding the offense, you are protecting your wounded heart, when just the opposite is true. Holding onto unforgiveness while waiting for justice only waters the seeds of bitterness that "grow up to cause trouble and defile many" (Heb. 12:15).

Unforgiveness strangles your ability to grow and over time, the heart withers up and becomes hardened, unable to give or receive love. Thinking you can wait to forgive until you are ready is self-deception. You will never feel like forgiving. It is a matter of your will to choose it.

You will need to give yourself grace. Forgiveness is a process that takes time. It acknowledges the feelings that accompany the offense and provides space to feel the pain and get out the hurt. Grieving losses such as the loss of innocence, loss of safety, and loss of dignity take time to release. Your time frame for mourning these losses is different in the same way as mourning the death of a loved one is particular to each person. Distressing memories must be sifted through and released as Jesus is welcomed in to touch painful places. Stages of grief in the midst of releasing forgiveness must be acknowledged and given time to work through for full release to occur.

Make no mistake, forgiveness is hard and it takes time. It may be something you have to choose every hour until you can do it every day, and as you choose forgiveness every day, the space between needing to ask yourself to forgive someone (even yourself) will get further and further apart.

WHAT FORGIVENESS IS NOT

Forgiveness is not forgetting what has happened or excusing the person for their behavior; rather, it is a choice to allow God into the wounded place with His healing presence. Giving the burden to Him to carry leaves no place for resentment to turn into bitterness. Justice demands action. Forgiveness releases the debt without demand, by taking the person off the hook and releasing them to God for justice. In the midst of His pain and agony on the cross, Jesus released his offenders to His Father when He said, "Father, forgive them, for they don't know what they're doing" (Lk. 23:34). Jesus knew that only the Father could pronounce judgment.

PRACTICE: PRAYER OF FORGIVENESS

Make a list of all the people you have to forgive and begin to walk through this process. Recognize that it will take time and repeated effort for you to fully let go of the offense. Don't be discouraged by this knowledge; rather, let it be an area where you ask God and others for help.

This prayer of forgiveness is a good starting point.

Lord Jesus, I know that you are with me, so I choose to forgive _____ (name the offender) for _____ (list the things the person did or failed to do) because it made me feel _____ (list all the painful feelings). I choose to release my pain to you and ask you to heal my damaged emotions. In Jesus' name, Amen.[26]

Are you ready to do the work? Be specific. Work through each person and each painful memory. In the presence of the Lord, other repressed feelings may surface that will need attention. Do not be discouraged by this process. It will end and you will be free.

---

[26] Neil T. Anderson, *The Steps to Freedom in Christ: A Biblical Guide to Help You Resolve Personal and Spiritual Conflicts and Become a Fruitful Disciple of Jesus* (Grand Rapids: Bethany House, 2017). For more on the topic of forgiveness, see Leanne Payne's *The Healing Presence: Curing the Soul Through Union With Christ* (Wheaton: Crossway Books, 1989) and *Restoring the Christian Soul: Overcoming Barriers to Completion in Christ Through Healing Prayer* (Grand Rapids: Baker Books, 1991).

You will recognize healing in your life when you recall painful memories and they no longer have the sting they once had upon mentioning them. Blessing the offender is another way to know that Jesus has healed you. You don't have to speak the blessing in person, but you can pray prayers of blessing for them in a genuine way, showing that you have released them into God's hands.

DISCUSSION QUESTIONS

1. *What do you think or feel to read, "Blessed are the broken, for theirs is the kingdom of heaven"?*

2. *What is an area of brokenness in which you struggle?*

3. *Look up Isaiah 53:3–5. What verbs are used to describe the brokenness of Jesus?*

4. *In the story of the two brothers, with which brother do you most relate and why?*

5. *How is your brokenness an obstacle to intimacy with God?*

6. *Which display of anger is most common for you (sarcasm, passive-aggressiveness, numbness, apathy, festering, or rage)?*

7. *Tell a story about a time when you acted out on your anger. Looking back, which of the six underlying emotional causes was really the issue (fear, invalidating your opinion, get out of my way, hurt, attacking your personhood, or unmet expectations)?*

8. *How does forgiveness play a role in dealing with anger in a healthy way? Who in your life do you need to forgive?*

Chapter 5.

INTIMACY: GOD'S DESIRE FOR ME

Thirsty hearts are those whose longings have been
wakened by the touch of God within them.[27]
—A. W. Tozer

How is your journey so far? I am so proud of you for making it this far with me. It's time for you to see how God desires to have intimacy with you through prayer and the reading of His Word. John 10:27 states, "My sheep listen to my voice; I know them and they follow me," indicating that you will recognize Him from all other voices.

The story is told of a man from America who went to visit his relatives in the Middle East. As shepherds, they gathered at a common well for their sheep to drink. The cousin was alarmed that the sheep would be mixed up because there was no branding on the sheep. The shepherd chuckled and told

---

[27] A. W. Tozer, *The Pursuit of God* (Aneko Press, Updated Edition, 2015), 17.

him not to worry, because they had a way to gather their sheep. After quite some time, the shepherds got up, said their good-byes, and walked away in different directions, each singing their favorite song. Upon hearing their shepherd, the sheep stopped eating, raised their heads, and began walking in that direction. Each sheep knew the voice of its master.

In the same way that we share secrets with our friends, God wants to share the secrets of his heart with us. He knows our secrets and our desires, and yet He wants us to share them with Him anyway. Our desire for intimacy is one of the indications that we have been made in God's image. Matthew 5:6 reminds us that "those who hunger and thirst for righteousness will be filled." Wesley Duewel described this desire when he wrote,

> Desire is another word for hunger. Unless there is sighing, longing, hungering and thirsting, and perhaps even tears of desire, you have probably not yet reached prevailing prayer. Unless your heart cries out from its hidden depths, Satan's roadblocks seem at times unmoved, and Satan's captives remain bound.[28]

Mirror Moment

Meditate on Psalm 63:1: "You, God are my God, earnestly I seek you; I thirst for you, my whole being longs for you." When you are ready, pray the following prayer: "God, will you increase my hunger for you?"

---

[28] Wesley Duewel, *Mighty Prevailing Prayer: Experiencing the Power of Answered Prayer* (Grand Rapids: Zondervan, 1990), 71.

INTENTIONALITY IS THE KEY

Intimacy does not occur haphazardly. Isaiah 50:4–5 reads,

> The Sovereign Lord has given me a well-instructed tongue, to know the word that sustains the weary. He wakens me morning by morning, wakens my ear to listen like one being instructed. The Sovereign Lord has opened my ears; I have not been rebellious, I have not turned away.

It is interesting that the writer made sure to say that he had not been rebellious or turned away after God opened His ears. Perhaps that is our first inclination when we hear so clearly what God is saying. Are we embarrassed by what is asked? Do we feel put on the spot that as the One who heard the message, we are therefore responsible to have to say it or do it? Do we have a whining attitude of why me? I don't want to do it! It's hard. What will people think? Will anybody listen to me?

According to this passage, God is waking us morning by morning to listen like one being instructed; therefore, He has specific information He wants us to receive. He is looking for men and women who will take seriously His words to them. Second Chronicles 16:9 reads, "The eyes of the Lord range to and fro throughout the Earth to strengthen those whose hearts are fully committed to Him." The psalmist wrote, "I have hidden your word in my heart that I might not sin against you" (Ps 119:11). Hiding God's word in our hearts keeps us tender toward Him and empowers us to know the word that sustains the weary.

EMBRACE AMBIGUITY

Are you demanding too much of yourself? Oftentimes in our relationship with God, we put demands on ourselves that are not from God. We feel we need to come into His presence to get something to give away to others, rather than just enjoy Him, worship Him, and be close to Him. Making time for God just to be in His presence is a sign of a secure relationship. In every relationship, there is the enjoyment of being together. There is usually conversation, but when it is quiet, the moment is simply enjoyed together. In those moments with God, we change our breathing to relaxation, focusing on His beauty and majesty, rather than on the next assignment. Simply being still before Him to know He is God is part of it. This is the place of peace. This is the place of breakthrough. This is the place of vision. There is no rush in this place, and not everything received here is meant to be shared with anyone else. It is your private place that no one else gets to enter. Much like the master bedroom for a married couple.

My husband and I have very busy ministry schedules. We often open our home and enjoy hanging out, eating food, and having a good time with our friends. People are free to move about the house and sit where they are comfortable, but there is one room off limits to guests—the master bedroom. That is the one place that is set apart for us alone. It is safe. It is restful. It is a place where love is expressed and received and meant for no one else.

Every encounter in the presence of the Lord will not be a fireworks explosion. Some of the most powerful encounters are quiet with tangible waves of peace or love. Other times have no feeling or expression that the person encounters, but a deep knowing that the word of God is true. It is during the times of quiet that negative thoughts are stirred up within us. Thoughts such as, "God doesn't care about me. This works for everyone else, but me. What is wrong with me? This is dumb. This is a waste of time." These are lies that must be unveiled and addressed. Such knowledge of these lies is a gift from God to help remove these obstacles and become more intimate with Him.

We are not aware that these lies exist, because they do not surface until God doesn't come to us in the way we think He should come. It is deep vulnerability to come to someone in love, only to have them jilt you. Rejection triggers abandonment issues and true feelings that are hidden below the surface that have no other way to be revealed than through silence and waiting. Fear is what causes people to avoid silence in the first place.

Waiting is not something we do well. We live in an instant society where whatever we want is at our fingertips. If we want information, we google it. If we are hungry, we use a microwave. If we want relationship, we text someone. Talking to someone face-to-face is less popular than even a few years ago, because of the time it takes to arrange a meeting. Why bother with that when I can stay in my pajamas on the couch and communicate on my phone? We have lost an integral part of intimacy that anticipates the face-to-face meeting. Imagine having a relationship with someone you never see, but only read their words to you. We were made for face-to-face encounters to enjoy one another's presence. God is speaking all the time, but some people have not yet recognized what He sounds like.

OBEY RIGHT AWAY

Years ago, I had a neighbor who never came on our side of the street. We waved to each other from the driveway or sidewalk, but she always stayed in her yard. Surprisingly, one Saturday while all four of my children were taking a nap, there was a knock on the door. When I opened it, Laura was standing there. I invited her in, made coffee, and we sat at the kitchen table to talk. As soon as I sat down, I "heard" a whisper tell me to share the gospel. I quickly pushed it aside and continued the conversation. After a few minutes passed, I heard it again. In my head, I talked back to the voice and said it was too soon to jump into such a dialogue with Laura, because I didn't want to scare her away.

I heard the statement even louder to share the gospel. In my head, I argued that such boldness didn't align with friendship evangelism principles that required a natural relationship before plunging into a gospel presentation. The voice didn't go away. It only increased in volume. After an hour passed, Laura got up and said she needed to get back home. I told her how much I enjoyed our time together and hoped she would come again soon. I walked her to the door, hearing the statement one last time, "Share the gospel."

As soon as the door closed, I felt the conviction of the Holy Spirit and realized I had passed up a great opportunity. I repented to the Lord and told Him I would make it right. I walked across the street, and as I got closer to the house, noticed why she had come over. The TV was loudly broadcasting a football game, and many men were cheering in the living room. They were so loud they couldn't even hear my knock, so I had to keep ringing the doorbell.

When Laura's boyfriend came to the door, he muted the TV and all eyes turned toward me. I apologized for interrupting the game and made my way across the room to sit beside Laura as all the men watched me. As I sat down, I timidly stammered that I wanted Laura to know how much God loved her. Once the word *God* was mentioned, the men sighed and turned back to the game. Laura leaned closer to me, got big tears in her eyes, and told me that she had once known the Lord, but had turned away from Him. She went on to say that someday she would probably return to Him.

Her boyfriend noticed her emotion and yelled to her to get the men some food, because she had already been gone for over an hour. I quickly got up and said I had to leave in case one of the kids woke up from their nap. I practically ran out of her house.

As I crossed the street, the magnitude of the encounter hit me hard. God had set me up. He had brought Laura to my distraction-free home to share the gospel with her. I didn't listen to the voice, because I didn't want to be embarrassed, since it was her first time in my home. I cared more about my awkwardness than about her and what God was asking me to do.

By this time, I was crying really hard and told the Lord from that day forward, I would do whatever He wanted, whenever He wanted, and I wouldn't wait or talk myself out of it. Deep down, I knew I had heard the voice of the Lord and I blatantly ignored it. I still get emotional when I share that story, because I wonder what would have happened if I had shared the gospel. Would Laura have come back to the Lord? My disobedience burned something in my heart that day regarding the voice of God. He does speak and I must listen right away, whether I look foolish or not. He chose me to talk to Laura, and I blatantly ignored his request.

I know it was God's voice I heard that day, because I was too chicken to share the gospel myself and Satan wouldn't have wanted me to do that. It is not always clear it is His voice, but it is necessary to measure what we hear with the written word of God, because God's spoken word will never violate the written Word. It takes practice to act on what we hear to clarify if it is God, our own desire, or the voice of the enemy.

When it is God, there is usually an obvious outcome or result that we could not make happen, such as emotion, agreement, or willingness to act or stop acting a certain way. If it is our own desire, nothing really comes of it and we come to the realization we were just pushing our own agenda. If it is Satan's voice, it is usually accompanied by feelings of condemnation, guilt, fear, accusation, shame, blame, torment, and harassment.

> God's spoken word will never violate the written word.

As straightforward as the message was, I still refused to listen. It takes time, practice, and trust to decipher the voice of God, but we can trust the Holy Spirit to guide us into truth. If we demand certainty before acting, that is sight, not faith. Romans 10:17 reads that "faith comes by hearing and hearing by the word of God."

In the Greek, the word here is *rhema*, which means "that which is or has been uttered by the living voice." Hearing comes by the "living voice" of God. Isaiah 55:11 reads, "So is my word that goes out from my mouth: it will not return to me empty, but will accomplish what I desire and achieve the purpose for which I sent it." We can trust the rhema of God. He wants us to know what He sounds like to deepen our relationship with Him.

CASE STUDY FROM THE LIFE OF DAVID

A beautiful picture of intimacy with God is displayed through the life of David. I Samuel 16 tells the story of how David became king. Samuel was told by God to stop mourning Saul and go to Bethlehem to anoint one of Jesse's sons. When Samuel arrived and saw the oldest son, Eliab, he thought he must be the one. God warned Samuel not to look at height or outward appearance because the Lord looks at the heart. Five more men came into the room, but none of them were the one God had chosen. Samuel asked Jesse if he had any more sons, and he said there was one more in the pasture tending the sheep. Samuel told him to go get the boy.

When David arrived, he was probably out of breath from running. He was told to stand in front of Samuel, oil was poured on his head, and Samuel pronounced him as the next king of Israel. As soon as Samuel was done, David was sent back to the pasture to resume his duties as shepherd. Jesse had not even thought enough of David to bring him before Samuel that day, yet he was God's choice for king.

It would be another fifteen years before David took the throne in Israel, but day in and day out, he faithfully cared for the flock right in front of him. There were many skills that David developed as he wrote songs and practiced his slingshot in the wilderness. During this time alone, David drew near to God and became familiar with His voice.

God has many things to teach us alone. It can be painful and lonely, but it is necessary for growth. For some reason, we don't learn it any other way. For all of us, there is a time when God takes us to a place of obscurity to show us that He is enough for us.

OBSTACLE: LIES

What lies have you told and what lies are you believing? One of the biggest obstacles to intimacy is lies. Lies are nasty little creatures that suck the life out of a person. They latch on to pain and create an unhealthy stronghold. When a person gets hurt, the lie is right there to snatch up the opportunity. Thoughts like, "I am alone. No one cares about me. I must do it myself" come rushing in and begin their torment. Such lies create a foundation on which we form our belief system.

We live by what we believe, so whatever the lie is, we are set up for unhealthiness. If we believe we must do everything ourselves, because we are alone and no one cares for us, we will not ask for help. If we believe we are worthless, we will not take the necessary risks to advance in our job, because we don't believe it will do any good. If we believe that this is as good as it gets, we won't dream for the future because there is no point. In these ways, lies not only prevent us from moving forward, but they replace truth. Truth is the key component to being set free.

When we believe the truth that God is with us, we seek the help we need, expecting to find it. When we believe we have worth, we take risks and don't worry about failure, because our identity is not wrapped up in our performance. We are still loved and that cannot be taken away.

If we have hope, we allow ourselves to dream of what could be. Such possibility thinking opens the avenue for creativity to flourish. Shame often attaches to the lie and leaves us feeling exposed and humiliated. Shame is not of God and nothing that makes us feel shameful or unworthy is ever from God. To really understand this, we have to understand better God's reality.

APPEARANCE VS. REALITY

David Benner, a Christian psychologist, wrote, "Focusing on God while failing to know ourselves deeply may produce an external form of piety, but it will always leave a gap between appearance and reality."[29] Perfectionism is a relentless taskmaster who demands more and more and more from us, but is never satisfied. It creates a huge gap between appearance and reality.

It will take years to peel back all the layers and identify our lies. There are still times when we feel worthless or useless and it touches a sore spot in our soul that wants to prove something. We want to prove that we are significant. We want to prove that we can outwork anyone. We want to prove that we are worth someone's time and attention. Freedom comes as we learn that our worth is not based on what we do; rather, our worth is based on what Jesus has done for us in bearing all our sin and shame on the cross. This grace is applied through faith in the One who bore our shame.

When we don't spend time with the Lord hearing the truth that He loves us as we are, we are easily offended and our need to prove ourselves returns. Our offenses revolve around feeling insignificant, unappreciated, unnoticed, and unaffirmed. The lies try to return and seem true because of experience and feelings. It is during such times that the Holy Spirit whispers that we are not alone because He is with us. He reminds us of what Jesus has done for us.

It is indeed a battle that is not against flesh and blood. Ephesians 6:12 reminds us that our battle and struggle are waged against the rulers of the darkness of this world. It starts in our mind and it starts with a lie. When we agree with the lie, we give it power in our lives.

---

[29] David Benner, *The Gift of Being Yourself* (Downers Grove: InterVarsity Press, 2004), 20–21.

We must be keenly aware of the truth so the lies are blatantly obvious and we immediately reject them when they come. It takes practice. There is a part of us that may want to wallow in self-pity, but it truly leads nowhere. Perspective is important and a slight adjustment from lies to truth changes everything.

It takes discipline to keep our thoughts on truth. Paul exhorts us to "be transformed by the renewing of our minds" (Rom. 12:2). The Greek word for transformed is *metamorphao*, meaning "from the inside out." The lie comes into our mind, but the transformation also occurs in our mind as we choose truth over lies.

Mirror Moment

Take a moment and think about the lies you believe. Make a list of them on the left side of the page. Don't feel badly if there is a long list. When you are ready, make a new column on the right side of the page and write a truth statement to replace each lie. Search for Bible verses that support your truth statements and write them beside the truth statements. This may take time. These truths need to become the new tape that plays in your mind when you believe the lies. Acknowledge each lie and its accompanying feeling, but replace it with the truth statement and Bible verse(s).

FALSE SELF

The false self is the person we create to cover up our feelings of worthlessness, shame, and inadequacy. Rather than being broken and admitting we need a savior and a healer, we pretend that we are fine as we are and don't need anyone or anything. Perhaps even worse is to pretend we do need others, but never really allow them to speak into our life. We attend events and are present physically, but emotionally we shut down and spiritually we only have the appearance of engagement. We walk in hurting and we walk out hurting because no one really knows what is going on.

Our mask is securely in place and we know the right phrases and clichés to say to back people off. "God is good," "I am blessed," and "I have so much to be thankful for" are statements that roll off our tongues, while our hearts are aching for true fellowship. Image is all-important; therefore, we cannot ruin that by showing others who we really are.

Success, people-pleasing, power, money, and even ministry can be used to cover up the false self. Benner wrote, "While other people's excessive attachments and personal falsity often seem glaringly apparent, it is never easy to know the lies of our own life."[30]

THE WAY THROUGH: DISCIPLINE OF HONESTY

As previously mentioned in chapter three, the church is called to be the community of truth who lives transparently. Silence causes inward destruction, but confession and forgiveness bring healing and freedom. Silence gives the sin nowhere to go, so it grows in our minds as we replay it again and again. Fueled by silence, negativity warrants a situation worse than it really is. The wildfire increases and sends us into a downward spiral of hopelessness and despair.

---

[30] Benner, *The Gift of Being Yourself,* 83

Once we speak what is bothering us—confess our sin—and bring it into the light, the reality of the situation returns to its normal size, lies are exposed, and truth enters. The situation may still be dire, but truth accesses light and our ability to handle what is there. God is given access by our confession. Speaking the truth to God allows Him to come in and grant us forgiveness. "If we confess our sins, he is faithful and just and will forgive us our sins and purify us from all unrighteousness" (I Jn. 1:9).

Telling the truth allows us to grow up and mature.

Telling the truth allows us to grow up and mature. "Speaking the truth in love, we will grow to become... mature" (Eph. 4:15). It is a choice. "Therefore, each of you must put off falsehood and speak truthfully to your neighbor, for we are all members of one body" (Eph. 4:25). The church needs to be the place in our culture where truth is spoken. "Therefore confess your sins to each other and pray for each other so that you may be healed. The prayer of a righteous man is powerful and effective" (James 5:16). Truth-telling requires discipline because it does not come naturally to us.

FREEDOM REQUIRES TRUTH

Everyone is broken and flawed. If we want to truly love others, we must present our real selves, just as we are—full of faults and flaws. Not only does this need to occur in order to receive the love we desperately crave, but it gives permission to others to do the same. Fear of rejection is so strong that many of us would rather go without love than expose our lies.

The mask has been on for so long, we don't remember what we really look like and the thin line between the lies we have believed and the truth of who we are has become too blurry. Only by walking in the light do we have fellowship with others (I Jn. 1:6–7). It doesn't mean perfection; rather, it means that truth is necessary if we are to experience love and forgiveness.

> Only by walking in the light do we have fellowship with others.

When we live in honesty, we choose for others to see our warts and all. It is vulnerable, but real. Many Christians walk around feeling lonely and depressed, because they are not presenting their true selves. They have picked up clues that being real is not acceptable, so they smile and swallow their pain.

AUTHENTIC CHURCH?

Some churches choose image over honesty. The way things appear are more important than the way things are. Outwardly everyone looks great and praises God, claiming everything we need God will do for us, but pretention is thick in the air, indicating authenticity isn't welcome. If we do share an emotional story of pain, others silently stare at us until we apologize for crying. Their silence speaks loud and clear that superficiality is the standard. Sometimes we do have momentary lapses of truth and our real self emerges, but a quick mask adjustment sends us back into hiding.

The church is challenged by authenticity, because once someone honestly and vulnerably shares their story, there is an expectation for the next person to tell their story and on and on. Honesty is feared, because it blows up the image of everything being okay. Honesty makes room for the raw mess, while image forces the mess to stay at the door. Image-conscious relationships remain shallow and church becomes an event to attend, rather than a place for broken people to come for healing.

HONESTY IN PRAYER

One of the best places for honesty is in prayer. It is the starting place to admit to God and ourselves our need for Him. Real praying can be a gut-wrenching process whereby the deep longings of our heart are admitted. Oftentimes it looks like a whine session of complaints, but we are being real about what is going on inside. This type of praying is exactly how David prayed in the Psalms, Jeremiah prayed in Lamentations, and Jesus prayed in the Garden of Gethsemane: "Please, Father, is there any other way for us to do this?"

In Matthew 26:36–46, Jesus asked, "Father, if it is possible, may this cup be taken from me." Jesus knew in His heart there was no other way, because He and the Father and the Holy Spirit had talked about it before Jesus came to earth, but Jesus asked anyway because He was revealing the fear, insecurity, and apprehension that accompanies every human being who is faced with something they know they must do, but dread it. This is honest praying.

Jesus said to his three best friends in verse 38: "My soul is overwhelmed with sorrow to the point of death. Stay here and keep watch with me." He told them how deeply He was hurting and invited them to join Him, but they didn't understand.

No matter how much He wanted someone with Him in this situation, He knew he must face it alone, but He still asked. He kept checking on the disciples to see if they were in it with him, but He found them sleeping. Three times He went away and prayed the same thing. The *same thing*. Why would He pray the same thing when He knew the answer?

Why do we pray the same thing when we know the answer? Because there is relationship in our asking. There is an intimacy we experience with God in the asking that allows us to ask even when we already know the answer. That is honesty. God is not upset that we keep asking the same thing over and over, because He knows we are processing our emotions as we wrestle with it and He gives us the freedom to come to our conclusion of either doing our own thing or saying, "Not my will, but yours be done."

God is secure in our relationship to allow us to be honest and make our own choice. Jesus knew His sole purpose for coming to earth was to do the will of the Father, but He had to be honest with how He truly felt as He faced death. Jesus' conclusion was submission to the Father, because He knew how much the Father loved Him. He wanted to please the Father because of the depth of their relationship.

Jesus was scared and knew He would be alone. He knew what his mission was, but He was still afraid. His example of gut-level, honest praying shows us that it is okay for us to pray like this too. Not everyone will decide to please the Father, but He gives everyone the freedom to honestly work it through and make their choice. Jesus understands what it is to wrestle in prayer. Wrestling in prayer is necessary, so when surrender is chosen, it is authentic.

PRACTICE: MEDITATION

Take a moment and read these verses from Psalms 32 and 62 several times.

> When I kept silent,
> my bones wasted away
> through my groaning all day long.
> For day and night
> my strength was sapped
> as in the heat of summer.
> Then I acknowledged my sin to you
> and did not cover up my iniquity.
> I said, "I will confess
> my transgressions to the LORD."
> And you forgave
> the guilt of my sin.
> (32:3–5)
> Trust in him at all times, you people;
> pour out your hearts to him,
> for God is our refuge. (62:8)

Are there things in your life that need to be spoken because your silence is slowly killing you inside? Take time and pour out your heart to Him.

Who else needs to be told so you will have the needed support to live in the light?

DISCUSSION QUESTIONS

1. *On a scale of one to ten, one being low and ten being high, how thirsty are you for more of God? Explain.*

2. How do you "listen like one being instructed" as mentioned in Isaiah 50:4–5?

3. Where is a safe place for you to be honest about what's really going on in your life?

4. What lies prevent you from drawing closer to God? Share the biggest lie you believe from the list you created in the Mirror Moment in this chapter.

5. In what way(s) have you ever heard God speak to you outside of the Bible (pictures, words, songs, nature, etc.)? Tell us your story.

6. Have you ever had a similar incident as Wanda had with Laura? Tell us your story.

Chapter 6.

MY IDENTITY IN CHRIST: FOSTERING MY RELATIONSHIP WITH JESUS

Define yourself radically as one beloved by God. This is the true self. Every other identity is illusion.[31]
—BRENNAN MANNING

If you have a driver's license or ID card, then you have experienced a photo of yourself that you probably don't care for. I would venture that most of us don't like the picture we had taken. "May I see your ID?" This is a dreaded but needed question when asked to prove we are who we say we are. Cashiers ask this question when a credit card is used to purchase an item. The customer with the credit card shows the cashier an

---

[31] Brennan Manning, *Abba's Child: The Cry of the Heart for Intimate Belonging* (Carol Stream: NavPress, 1997), 59.

official photo ID, like a driver's license, to prove that the person holding the card matches the picture on the card.

This identification is proof that we are who we say we are. Although cashiers are supposed to ask to see ID every time a credit card is used, many are in such a rush to move on to the next customer they don't even bother. Identity theft is on the rise as thieves are intentionally seeking to misuse someone's personal identifying information for their own financial gain.

It is very appealing to steal someone else's identity, because it can easily be done electronically. A person with strong computer skills can "hack" into someone's account to acquire confidential banking information and begin using the numbers from those accounts to make online purchases. Banks set up security systems to identify suspicious purchases to keep accounts protected. Such protection denies the use of the card if fraud is suspected.

This is so close to what it is like when we pretend to be someone else and stay in the falsehood of our lies. It is a bold act to pretend to be someone else, but at times all of us present ourselves one way, when inside we are totally different. In the movie *Mona Lisa Smile* a colleague began a romantic relationship with Julia Roberts' character. He allowed those around him to believe he had been in the war in Europe when he had been stationed on Long Island, New York. He commented to Roberts, "I just never corrected them." She was devastated at his deception and lack of character and immediately became suspicious about their relationship, wondering if he had lied about other things. He went on to say she made it hard for someone to be honest with her, because she had such high expectations and standards. Instead of owning his own wrongdoing, he turned it on her. His lying was *her* fault. How crazy!

It's easier to let people think well of us and not correct them than expose our fraudulence.

Deflection and blame are common responses when we are caught in a lie. It's easier to let people think well of us and not correct them than expose our fraudulence. We don't lie directly; rather, we let the moment pass silently to avoid supposed awkwardness by correcting the misinformation. In reality, our silence secures our mask, cementing the incongruence between our inner self and outer appearance, making it more difficult to speak up the next time.

Mirror Moment

Take a moment and journal about a time when you have allowed people to believe something about you that was false. Why didn't you correct them?

JESUS' MISSION

Jesus knew who He was. In Luke 2, when He was twelve years old, His parents couldn't find him on a trip back to Nazareth after observing Passover in Jerusalem. Three days later, they found Him in the temple courts sitting among the teachers and asking them questions. Everyone who heard Him was amazed at his understanding and his answers.

When His parents found him, they were astonished, yet felt disrespected that Jesus hadn't let them know where He was. Jesus replied in verse forty-nine, "Why were you searching for me?" He asked. "Didn't you know I had to be in my Father's house?" Mary and Joseph didn't understand what He was saying to them, but Jesus went with them while Mary treasured those things in her heart. It would be eighteen more years before Jesus became public in His teachings.

In John 5:19, Jesus responded to the Jewish leaders that "the Son can do nothing by himself; he can do only what he sees his Father doing, because whatever the Father does the Son also does." In John 14:31, Jesus declared that the prince of this world has no hold over Him, but He comes "so that the world may learn that I love the Father and do exactly what my Father has commanded me."

Jesus knew He had come to earth to represent the Father. In John 17:25–26, Jesus prayed, "Righteous Father, though the world does not know you, I know you, and that you have sent me. I have made known to them and will continue to make you known in order that the love you have for me may be in them and that I myself may be in them." Jesus had a clear sense of mission.

JESUS' BLESSING

A story is told of a father who paused the celebration of his son's bar mitzvah to have his son take a seat in the center of the room. The father then called over all the men to surround them. The father then placed his hands on his son's shoulders and loudly pronounced, "This is my son, whom I love; with him I am well pleased. Welcome him into the company of men!"

The people in the room shouted and hollered their approval of the boy who had just crossed over into manhood. It is interesting to ponder if such an occasion happened in Jesus' life. Would the scandalous details surrounding His birth regarding the identity of His "real" father have made it uncomfortable for the family to have such a ceremony? God Himself decided to clear up the rumors about Jesus' identity. Upon coming out of the waters of baptism, God declared for all to hear that Jesus was His beloved Son, on whom His favor rests. Talk about a rite of passage into manhood!

Jesus' ministry did not begin until He received the blessing from the Father. Jesus did not do anything *for* acceptance. He acted from acceptance. Knowing His Father loved Him provided the security He needed to live authentically.

> Jesus did not do anything *for* acceptance. He acted from acceptance.

In the first phrase, God gave His child acceptance, declaring, "This is my son." God was proud to call Jesus Son and admitted that Jesus belonged to Him. God accepted *all* of whom Jesus was. The statement was made publicly before witnesses, but I believe God did it in large part just for Jesus. The amount of rejection Jesus was going to encounter leading to His death would cause self-doubt to arise along with the desire to go an easier way. Now Jesus would have this experience to recall what his Father said about who He was.

In the second phrase, *whom I love*, God announced his affection. This declaration was a powerful statement of God's emotion, care, and love for Jesus. As a parent, love for children is assumed. Children will sometimes say, "But you have to say that, you're my dad." What they don't understand is that a parent doesn't have to say I love you, they *get* to say I love you. There is no greater joy than to tell your child you love him or her, and it is fully received. God the Father unashamedly let the whole world know that He deeply loved Jesus.

In the final phrase, *with you I am well pleased*, God spoke of His approval. God's statement was not weak in any way.

There was no hint of mistrust or unbelief. God did not say, "Give him a chance; see what you think about him; he's got a lot to learn, but he's a good guy." God's statement of Jesus was strong and definitive.

The phrase *this is my Son* removed all doubt about his heritage. The phrase *whom I love* left no question where God's love, devotion, and loyalty lay. *With you I am well pleased* signified God's seal of approval. Nothing establishes our identity like our father's love.

When we are unsure of our father's acceptance, affection, and approval, we tend to look for it in other places or worse yet, put on a mask and pretend to be someone we are not to get our emotional needs met. This is the worst thing we can do because people will end up loving the mask instead of the real us, because they don't know the real us. Not only will we end up feeling isolated and alone, still longing for acceptance, love, and approval, but we will not be able to receive it because an imposter has taken over our persona.

> Removal of the mask and presenting our true selves is the only hope we have of being truly loved.

We play the part of a character in our own narrative that isn't us. Our false self is all that people know. Removal of the mask and presenting our true selves is the only hope we have of being truly loved. Initially the mask feels safe, enabling a person to hide to prevent rejection, but eventually the loneliness is overwhelming. David Benner wrote,

> At some point in childhood we all make the powerful discovery that we can manipulate the truth about our-

selves. Initially it often takes the form of a simple lie—frequently a denial of having done something. But of more importance to the development of the false self is the discovery that our ability to hide isn't limited to what we say or don't say. We learn to pretend. We discover the art of packaging our self.[32]

The scary part of packaging our self is that what started as a role can become an identity. We lose sight of reality and what we really think and feel in our heart. Fears of being found out, less than, and not good enough rear their ugly heads and the possibility of rejection keeps us silent and suffering alone.

The great sadness in living a fake life is that no one knows the real you. Anxiety and depression may eventually surface because of the incongruence. Benner goes on to say that "the only hope for unmasking the falsity that resides at the core of our being is a radical encounter with truth."[33]

GET REAL

Are you ready to be you? Living from the true self means no more pretension. Coming out of hiding and receiving love takes vulnerability. There is a children's story by Margery Williams called *The Velveteen Rabbit* in which the Skin Horse and Rabbit are talking about becoming real.

> "Real isn't how you are made," said the Skin Horse. "It's a thing that happens to you. When a child loves you for a long, long time, not just to play with, but REALLY loves you, then you become Real."

---

[32] David Benner, *The Gift of Being Yourself* (Downers Grove: IVP, 2004), 78.
[33] Benner, *The Gift of Being Yourself*, 79.

The Skin Horse goes on to ask if it happens all at once or bit by bit.

"It doesn't happen all at once," said the Skin Horse. "You become. It takes a long time. That's why it doesn't often happen to people who break easily, or have sharp edges, or who have to be carefully kept. Generally, by the time you are Real, most of your hair has been loved off, and your eyes drop out and you get loose in the joints and very shabby. But these things don't matter at all, because once you are Real you can't be ugly, except to people who don't understand."[34]

Love has the power to change people. Pretention fades away and who we really are is received and deemed acceptable by us because the person loving us knows the real us.

Accepting who we are with our flaws, warts, and weaknesses is a first step in recognizing we need a savior to save us from ourselves. Self-rejection is a powerful enemy of God's intention. "The penetration of our delusions is enormously challenging. It requires a relentless commitment to truth and a deep sense of freedom from fear of rejection. Nothing facilitates this like the knowledge of being deeply loved."[35]

> **Love has the power to change people.**

God loves us just as we are and our identity is established by security in this kind of love. Once the mask of the false self is removed, there is freedom to receive acceptance, affection,

---

[34] Margery Williams, *The Velveteen Rabbit* (New York: Doubleday, 1922), 5.
[35] M. Basil Pennington, *True Self/False Self: Unmasking the Spirit Within* (New York: Crossroad, 2000), 31.

and approval. This gift of acceptance is ours to claim. All of mankind has a longing and legitimate emotional need to experience such love.

King Solomon wrote in Song of Songs 8:7, "Many waters cannot quench love." Love has caused many a valiant warrior to fight for the hand of a beautiful maiden. Love is what caused Jesus to be willing to die such a violent death in order for mankind to be reconciled to God. It's time to stop hiding behind our mask and receive the extravagant love of God. It will transform us from the inside out and establish our identity in Christ.

OBSTACLE: FEAR

When I was in elementary school, there was an older heavyset neighborhood girl who would sneak up behind me, pin my arms, and put her hand over my mouth and nose to smother me. She would hold me for a few seconds, then push me away, laughing as I gasped for air. She made sure this only happened when we were alone. She never did this when my older brothers and sister were around.

One summer night, several of us were playing hide and go seek and she was "it." I made it safely to base and instead of finding the other kids who were hiding, she once again pinned me and held her hand over my nose and mouth for a long time. I wriggled to get free and pulled at her hand, but she held on. Panic set in, and I grabbed her hand with both of mine and dug my fingernails into her skin as hard as I could. She pushed me to the ground, screaming that I had made her bleed.

She ran off, threatening to call my father to tell him what I had done. I ran into the house to pick up the phone just as it rang. It was her, demanding that I let her speak to my father. I pleaded with her not to tell my dad. She had twisted the story to make me the bad guy. I absolutely should have let her talk to my father, but I was afraid and manipulated into believing I was wrong and would get in trouble for hurting her.

To this day, if someone comes up behind me and puts their hands over my eyes to guess who they are, I instinctively push their hands away, whip around, and tell them not to do that to me. They usually think I'm overreacting, but have no idea what is triggered in me by that "innocent" game. No matter what I know cognitively about their playfulness, my experiential knowledge kicks in that I am in potential danger. I am not alone.

According to the National Institute of Mental Health, 10 percent of people in the US, approximately 9.7 million people, experience phobias, many caused by some kind of trauma. Phobias are the most common mental disorders in the US, affecting women more than men and include anxiety disorders, panic disorders, post-traumatic stress disorders, and obsessive-compulsive disorders.[36]

DEFINITION OF FEAR

Fear can be defined as an unpleasant emotion caused by the belief that someone or something is dangerous and likely to cause pain or injury. If fear is caused by a belief, then it can be overcome by changing one's thinking. This is much easier said than done.

---

[36] https://www.verywellmind.com/prevalence-of-phobias-in-the-united-states-2671912.

In a study of thirty thousand adults who reported high stress levels, only those who *believed* that stress was harmful met an early death. Stress was not the villain—it was the fear that stress was harmful that was the danger.[37] Adults call fear depression, anxiety, stress, nervousness, or tension. Children call it being scared or afraid and are simple and direct in their expression of emotions, stating they are mad, sad, glad, or scared.

They know they live in a world they can't control, whereas adults feel they should overcome fear, so they get angry for its arrival and refuse to accept their inability to control it. Calling fear stress and blaming the person or situation that triggered the feeling never addresses the fear itself.

Parents' and caregivers' responses to situations let children know if something is safe. If the caregiver freaks out, runs to the child's aid to remove him from danger, and screams at the child to get off the wall or get away from the fire, the child learns from the caregiver's reaction how to respond in those situations. If the caregiver smiles when they see the child, calmly cautions the child to be careful, or joins in with the child, the child learns discretion, but not fear.

There is little to no sense of adventure with a fearful person, because every possible thing that could go wrong is stated as an objection to the venture. For most people, a simple checklist of pros and cons is quickly tallied and the decision is made to proceed. Phobics are not so easily persuaded and withdraw from potential danger.

------

[37] http://blogs.edweek.org/edweek/next_gen_learning/2019/02/the_upside_of_stress.html.

Fear is caused by a belief that starts in the mind. The apostle Paul exhorted the Philippians, "Whatever is true, noble, right, pure, lovely, admirable, excellent, praiseworthy—think about such things" (Phil. 4:8–9). If thoughts are confined to these areas, there is no room for fear.

> Fear is caused by a belief that starts in the mind.

Look how different our outlook is if we think about whatever is false, vulgar, wrong, impure, ugly, reprehensible, inferior, or degrading. Paul knew people's tendency to think negatively and had to tell them to think the opposite. This is the place where fear, shame, and unbelief enter. "What if" scenarios play countless scenes in the mind, and lies bombard one's thinking. It is agreement with such lies that opens the door to fear, because fear is a belief that danger, harm, or injury will come to us. This belief is not necessarily true, but at times, our response to the possibility causes us to act in ways that bring on the very thing we are most afraid of happening. We have to rewire the way we think if we are going to think more like Paul and less like the world.

REINFORCING FEAR

Robert Rosenthal defined the Pygmalion effect as "the phenomenon whereby one person's expectation for another person's behavior comes to serve as a self-fulfilling prophecy."[38]

Parents do not realize the extent to which their expectations influence their children's behavior. People who get the

---

[38] Robert Rosenthal, "Self-Fulfilling Prophecy and the Pygmalion Effect in Management," *American Psychologist* 58.3 [November 2003], 839.

attention live up to the expectations of the influencer, be it a parent, leader, coach, or teacher. This works positively and negatively. Children with "potential" get positive attention, extra time, affirmation, and encouragement.

Parents console their children when they get hurt, kiss the scrape, and put them back in the game, sending the message that they can handle the situation and don't need to be afraid. On the other hand, children expected to act out or perform poorly do not disappoint. These children receive less attention or little to no affirmation for their efforts, are given labels, causing them to withdraw, and perform at the low level of expectation. A thought builds on itself and the smallest movement in the same direction turns a snowball into an avalanche—all starting with one's thinking.

Parents' statements become a curse upon the child and a way of manipulating him or her to do what the parent wants. Statements like "you can't do that, you're too (fill in the blank—skinny, tall, slow, fat, etc.)" stifle the ability of the person hearing the statement, because they *believe* the person who said it. The person surmises that if their mom, dad, big brother or sister, teacher, principal, pastor, or coach think that is the case, it must be true.

Sometimes such statements cause a person to dig deep and prove that person wrong, but most of the time, such negative attention and statements kill the joy of a person from wanting to try and enforce a fear of failure. Words matter.

Mirror Moment

Take a moment and reflect on the way in which your parents talked to you about risk. Were you encouraged to play it safe or be adventurous? Bullet list your fears.

FEAR'S IMPACT UPON SPIRITUALITY

How is fear impacting your spiritual walk? Fear impacts spirituality in three ways. The first way is that fear demands sight. A hypervigilance is created to foresee potentially dangerous moments and to avoid them at all costs. Anxiety or anger develops when something unexpected happens and God does not intervene.

There is an expectation on the part of the follower that God's guidance will show His children the way around obstacles. Just the opposite is true. Faith goes *through* difficulties, because of its confidence in what is hoped for and assurance of what is unseen (Heb. 11:1).

The second impact of fear upon spirituality is that fear demands understanding. A hypervigilance of analysis is created to figure things out to remain safe. Risks are small and calculated and frustration sets in when God cannot be understood or doesn't cooperate with one's demands. Faith embraces ambiguity and is fine to live with uncertainty until God chooses to reveal it. It takes on a curious attitude of wondering how God will get us through each circumstance, but it is relaxed with the unknown, realizing that God will reveal His strategy in perfect timing.

The third impact of fear upon spirituality is that fear demands control. An obsession to control is created, leaving no room for God to be God. Faith trusts God and His ways while learning to surrender control and wait for His guidance while holding to His promise to never leave or forsake us. Fear is a crippler that paralyzes God's children.

Faith recognizes risk, but trusts God to handle each hardship and bring understanding when the time is right. In the meantime, the person holds steady, because of the faithful track record of God. All pressure is removed from the person to make something happen, because the person is not in control. He or she waits in faith, trusting God to reveal each part in His way and in His timing. "For the Spirit God gave us does not make us timid, but gives us power, love and self-discipline" (II Tim. 1:7).

FACE THE FEAR

It is important to identify the cousins of fear, which include the forms of anxiety, worry, intimidation, and self-doubt. Each of these forms carries with it the belief that we will not be able to do what is asked of us in the given situation. Thus pain or injury may come to us or those around us as a result. Once again, the false belief must be identified and replaced with truth, since none of these forms of fear produce anything positive.

Anxiety focuses on future events that may never occur. Worry torments with disturbing thoughts. Self-doubt lacks confidence in one's own motives. Intimidation pushes back through force of personality or anger. When any form of fear comes, it is necessary to feel it and not bolt.

FEEL IT

Remain still, take a deep breath, and feel the terror, anxiety, panic, apprehension, foreboding, or dread in whatever form it comes. Notice how your heart is racing, your breath is shallow, sweat just broke out on your upper lip, your stomach is in knots, tears started flowing, and any other physical reactions that occur. Your body is responding to your belief that you are powerless.

Purposely begin to take deep cleansing breaths. Inhale, hold for three seconds, and exhale slowly through the mouth. Repeat this a few more times, noticing your ability to think more clearly. As you remain still, speak out short statements like "I'm ok, I'm safe here, nothing here can hurt me, I am deeply loved by God, I am stronger than I think, I'm gonna make it." The feeling will subside, but you will need to wait it out for two or three minutes. This will seem like a long time, but it will pass.

Speak out loud the statements you believe and have prepared ahead of time. "The Lord is my light and my salvation. The Lord is the stronghold of my life. I will wait for the Lord, be strong and take heart and wait for the Lord" (Ps. 27:1, 14). These statements can be kept on your phone or on sticky notes, so when fear is triggered in you, there is a place for you to refer to them for support.

TALK ABOUT IT

Where in your life do you feel overwhelmed? Does this happen mostly at home, in your car, in your office, at school, at a friend's house, at a bar, at church, or at the mall? Speaking about the fear diminishes its power in your mind. Left to ruminate on, your thoughts careen out of control and your body releases the fear through anxiety or panic attacks. Remaining still to feel the fear and take authority over your thoughts will require discipline on your part.

You are breaking habits and patterns of response that will initially take effort. But soon, these new habits and response patterns will be the norm. Add to your statement list when you do not feel fear, so you are encouraged and strengthened in your beliefs. When fear strikes, you will only have to speak out these prepared statements that you know are true.

You are in a spiritual battle, and "your enemy, the devil, prowls around like a roaring lion looking for someone to devour" (I Pet. 5:8). You will no longer be one of his victims! "Resist him, standing firm in the faith, because you know that the family of believers throughout the world is undergoing the same kind of sufferings" (v. 9).

THE WAY THROUGH: DISCIPLINE OF SPIRITUAL WARFARE

We are in a spiritual battle and must be aware of the schemes that are used against us. Our focus is on God, but we need to be wise and aware of how our enemy operates. Satan uses any means to destroy us. We must recognize it is him so we will fight back. But our strategy against Satan is the opposite of how the world wages war.

The world has an anything goes mentality whereby you can do whatever you want to get your way—greed, lying, stealing, cheating, and deceiving are the norm. In the kingdom of God, war is waged through alignment with God, surrender to His lordship, and obedience to follow His commands. The weapons used are the gifts and fruit of the Spirit—love, joy, peace, patience, gentleness, goodness, meekness, faith, and self-control. These seem like unlikely characteristics for battle, but partnered with the power of God, they are unstoppable. The Lord is fighting our battles. We just hold His hand and keep in step with His Spirit.

When you said yes to God and surrendered your life to follow Him, your name was written on the top of the enemy's hit list. He knew that if you used the authority you had been given as a son or daughter of God, he would have to obey you. He does NOT want to obey you. He wants to destroy your life. Since the moment of your conception, he and his minions have plotted to destroy your life. "When he lies, he speaks his native language, for he is a liar and the father of lies" (Jn. 8:44).

GIVE UP OR SHUT UP

Satan's two strategies are to get you to give up or shut up, because he knows he must obey your command and surrender to the power and authority in the name of Jesus. Think about this again. You have power and authority in the name of Jesus. Your enemy knows this, so he hopes to keep you mired in lies and deception so you will continue to be ruled by fear.

"Through the praise of children and infants, you have established a stronghold against your enemies, to silence the foe and the avenger" (Ps. 8:2). Knowing he is already defeated, Satan must convince Jesus' followers to give away their authority. He does this by twisting the truth and making it appear true so you agree with his lies and give away your authority. Bit by bit, the lie moves from a foothold to a stronghold.

Agreement with the lie gives it a place in your mind, which is why you must "take every thought captive and make it obedient to Christ" (II Cor. 10:5). If you give up, Satan has won, because you sideline yourself and refuse to use the power and authority you have been given, believing it doesn't do any good. Be aware of this scheme.

The second strategy to get you to shut up is also important for your awareness. Satan knows that speaking out your resistance, rebukes, commands, and renunciations and declaring your purpose and alignment with Jesus is enough to defeat him. **In the name and authority of the Lord Jesus Christ, he**

must obey! This is the very reason "we pray in the Spirit on all occasions with all kinds of prayers and requests" (Eph. 6:18). Words matter.

The apostle Paul said, "Pray also for me, that whenever I speak, words may be given me so that I will fearlessly make known the mystery of the gospel… Pray that I may declare it fearlessly, as I should (Eph. 6:19-20). Why does he use the word *fearlessly* twice here? Because it's scary to stand up against the hordes of hell. Often resistance to the work of God comes in the form of a disagreeing teammate, or leader, or friend, or family member. Our battle is not against flesh and blood, but the enemy often plays on the fear of people to resist the work of God that is not seen, understood, or able to be con-

> Our battle is not against flesh and blood.

trolled. Beware of this scheme, resist it, and unite with your teammates to go after the real enemy!

The enemy's strategy to defeat you is to convince you to give up and shut up; therefore, you must stand up and speak up. Ephesians 6 has clear directives to be strong in the Lord and in his mighty power, put on the full armor of God, and stand against the devil's schemes. Specifically, Paul says, "Therefore put on the full armor of God, so that when the day of evil comes, you may be able to stand your ground, and after you have done everything, to stand" (v. 13).

BENEFITS OF JOURNALING

Are you writing your thoughts down? Journaling is a good exercise because it allows a person to freely write anything that comes to mind. It helps to articulate emotion that is churning inside by recording the date, day, and time of what God said so you are able to go back to it as often as possible as a remembrance of God's faithful word to you.

It is a record of your emotional state, naming the issue at hand and allowing God to speak into those moments with his truth and promises. It is an exercise of faith to put in writing what is happening in your life. The situation becomes real when it is committed to paper. In your head, you can let things whirl around and remain safe, but once you put it in print, it's open season for scrutiny. Even though you are incredibly particular with whom you share it, there is still deep vulnerability in getting it out and the possibility that another person will not be tender with your fragile heart.

You don't have to be an amazing writer to put your thoughts on paper. Journaling brings clarity as you articulate what is going on in your heart and mind. Writing clears the way for honest evaluation and ownership of your viewpoint. It can become a regular practice to record your thoughts, feelings, and prayers.

Another good practice is to pause after writing out your thoughts and feelings and ask the Lord if He has anything to say about the situation. This is called prophetic journaling. Write what comes to mind without censoring anything or determining if it is theologically correct. In making room for God, you can learn that He does speak and wants to speak into the intricate places of your life. You can read your entries to a trusted friend to see if they agree that it is God speaking. Sometimes parts will sound like God, but other parts will sound like your own insecurities or your family's view. Through this process, you will be able to figure out what God sounds like to you, enabling you to grow in your understanding of His voice in your life.

PRACTICE: JOURNALING

Find a quiet place and take a journal or notebook and pen. Write out your prayers or feelings to the Lord. When you finish, pause and ask the Holy Spirit if there is anything He wants to say to you or show you at this time. Write what comes to mind. Find a trusted friend, mentor, or loved one to whom you can read your entry. Discuss God's voice in the Bible and ask them how they discern what is God's voice and what is their own thoughts or feelings.

DISCUSSION QUESTIONS

1. *On a scale of one to ten, one being low and ten being high, where are you with taking risks? Explain.*

2. *How does your family handle fear?*

3. *What are your three biggest fears?*

4. *In what ways does your desire to see, understand, and control impact your spirituality?*

5. *Which of the fear responses is most common for you? Fight, flight, freeze, or submit?*

6. *What do you most commonly do to distract yourself from fear?*

7. *What is your best strategy to overcome fear?*

8. *Tell us a story of a time when you packaged yourself one way to others, when inside you were completely different? Why did you do that?*

9. *We all tend to have an image of ourself that we think makes us special. To what image may you be clinging (athlete,*

scholar, business associate, friend, helper, ministry leader, etc.)? Explain.

10. *In what ways does love have power?*

11. *How are God's acceptance, affection, and approval shaping your identity?*

Chapter 7.

HEARING GOD'S VOICE: "IS THAT YOU, GOD?"

God speaks in the silence of the heart.
Listening is the beginning of prayer.[39]
—MOTHER TERESA

Have you heard God speaking to you? If not, are you ready to hear Him? We serve a speaking God so we can expect to know what He sounds like. Some people get nervous when we talk about hearing God's voice, when in reality, "if we, though we are evil, know how to give good gifts, how much more will our Father in heaven give the Holy Spirit to those who ask him!" (Lk. 11:13). We open ourselves up to a God who is actively present in every detail of our lives, so understanding His Word to us is a natural part of the relationship. The Bible is the

---

[39] Laurie Watson Manhardt and Jan Liesen, *Wisdom: Job, Proverbs, Ecclesiastes, Song of Solomon, Wisdom, Sirach* (Steubenville: Emmaus Road Publishing, 2009), 205.

primary way God speaks to us, but we also learn to discern His voice outside of the Bible.

On the spiritual journey, connection with God by speaking and listening is called prayer. We talk to a God we cannot see, because He loves us and wants to connect with us. He is excited to hear about the details of our day and the places where we need His help. He is delighted to watch from a distance until He is invited closer.

Prayer is as simple as talking to a friend. It can be done silently or out loud. We can use prayer books or pray directly from our heart, saying what is on our mind in that moment. God has chosen prayer as the agency by which He connects with His children and accomplishes His purposes.

It is important to note here that just because we ask God for something, it doesn't mean we will get our way. God knows what is best for us. He is not our personal assistant or fairy godmother required out of obligation to fulfill our every whim and desire. As a father, he knows that if He allowed us to receive some things now, they would destroy us or ruin our relationship with Him. Sometimes He takes a long time to answer our requests, but there may be a few reasons for delays.

A delay can reveal a character issue and show us what is in our hearts, allowing us to recognize the selfishness of our request. A delay can also reveal that we are not quite ready or that things are not fully in place so we cannot step into the next thing. A delay reveals our depth of trust in God. When we are told to wait and respond with a temper tantrum or walk away from God, we are trying to take Him hostage and manipulate Him into giving us what we want. He will never fall for that. Waiting always exposes our heart. Talking, listening, and waiting are all necessary parts of communicating with a God we cannot see.

HOW CAN WE HEAR GOD?

There are several ways to "hear" God's voice. Our senses are involved in each of these ways, so what we hear, think, feel, see, or sense are all included under the umbrella of God's voice. In the Bible, God spoke in many ways: through a burning bush (Exodus 3), a gentle whisper (I Kings 19), and fingers of a human hand appearing and writing on a wall (Daniel 5). A donkey spoke to its master (Numbers 22), three men fell to the ground when they heard a voice from a cloud (Matthew 17), and a man experienced a light flash around him, he fell to the ground, heard a voice, and was struck blind for three days (Acts 9). In each of these instances, God spoke the way the person or people needed to hear so they would recognize it was Him. God is the same and is still speaking to us in ways for us to recognize that it is Him.

Hearing God is a normal part of the Christian life, but we have been taught that we can only "hear" through the Bible. The Bible is a primary way of hearing God, but there is more. How does a person decide who to marry? They will never find a place in Scripture with the person's name. How does a person decide what job to take or what college to attend or where to move? The guidance of the Lord is both through the written Word of Scripture (*logos*) and the spoken-now word (*rhema*). The rhema word is a particular now word of the Lord for a certain time, place, person, and need. What a person hears by the spoken word (*rhema*) will not contradict the written Word (*logos*); rather, it will align with the ways of God. God is the same yesterday, today, and forever (Heb. 13:8) and is still speaking to us in ways for us to recognize that it is Him.

Words of Knowledge and Words of Wisdom

These ways of hearing are called words of knowledge and words of wisdom. They are listed as spiritual gifts in I Corinthians 12. A word of knowledge is a supernaturally given piece of information or knowledge that could not have been known otherwise. A word of wisdom is supernaturally given application to a situation. Oftentimes we don't know that what we are hearing is the Lord's voice; rather, we credit it as good intuition. Here are eight descriptions of ways these words come to us to hear God, followed by an illustration of how these words can be used to pray for others.

Words or Phrases

The first way of hearing is a word or phrase. Sometimes we can see the word or phrase in our mind's eye—like the bubble of a comic strip revealing a person's thought or speech. At other times, the word or phrase is heard or seen on a person's body.

A few years ago, I was attending a conference and saw an acquaintance. We chatted briefly, but I could tell she wanted to keep things superficial and end the conversation. The next session, I saw her again, and she averted her eyes when she saw me. In the third session, when I saw her across the room, I saw the word *disappointment* in capital letters going down the side of her body. I approached her and since she had blown me off the two previous times, her guard was down. I told her what I saw and asked if I could pray for her. She got big tears in her eyes and said that it was her son, and she felt such shame because of his behavior and did not want me to think less of her. She was hurting and would not have said anything to me if I hadn't "heard" from the Lord and asked to pray for her.

Pictures

A second way of hearing God's voice is by seeing a picture. Sometimes there is a sense of what the picture means. At other times, the detailed description is a familiar place or an immediate understanding of the object described. It is important to gently and lovingly say what you are seeing, even if you don't know what it means, because you don't know the meaning it might have for the person receiving prayer.

There have been times when praying for women that I see a little girl crying in a place, and when I describe the picture, the woman I am praying for starts sobbing. When I pause to ask her what the Lord is doing, she reveals that the place I described was where she would go each time after she was abused. She continues to reveal that she has never told anyone about her abuse and now believes that God has shown it to a stranger so she can receive healing

Visions

A third way of hearing by way of a vision is similar to a picture, except there is movement. It's as if watching a movie trailer or short YouTube video. Simply describe the scene.

Bible Verses

A fourth way of hearing God is through Scripture. A Bible verse or reference pops into our mind and we can either recite the verse, paraphrase it, or look it up on our phone in a Bible app. For example, the word *fear* comes to mind, immediately followed by II Timothy 1:7. Say, "The word fear comes to mind and it reminds me of the verse in II Timothy that says, 'God has not given us a spirit

> The point of the prayer time is for the person to feel God's love.

of fear, but of love and power and a sound mind.'" The point of the prayer time is for the person to feel God's love. Praying in a low-key, casual way normalizes that God speaks.

Songs

A fifth way of hearing God is through music or songs. Sometimes people who have suffered long-term abuse "hear" God this way, because the music is able to penetrate the self-protective places of their heart. The music is not always a hymn or worship song. It is simply another way in which God lets the person know He is intricately involved in his or her life.

If you are a singer, you can sing what you are hearing. The song may be a song that means a lot to the person receiving prayer or the words of the song speak to the person's pain or situation. I have heard a tune in my head and then seen words in my mind's eye as if they were on a ticker tape. I realize the words match the cadence of the tune, so I sing what I hear and see, so when the words stop, I stop singing. It is usually very meaningful to the person receiving prayer.

Pain in Your Body

A sixth way of hearing God is through pain in your body. This can be missed as just our own aches and pains, and it takes discernment to realize it is an indication to pray for someone else. Many times, when praying for others, I have laid my hand on their shoulder and immediately felt despair, deep depression, or suicide. I was fine before touching them and had none of those intense feelings. I began to pray exactly what I felt until I didn't feel it anymore. The person receiving prayer usually becomes very emotional, since the person praying is describing exactly what the other person feels.

On another occasion, my husband and I were speaking at a church and I had a sharp pain to the left of my right shoulder blade. I thought it was from the way I was sitting, so I corrected my posture. Soon the muscle tightened and began to spasm, causing much pain. We were teaching on how to hear God's voice, but it didn't occur to me that this pain was connected to the teaching time.

Finally, it dawned on me that this was a word of knowledge, so I asked anyone in the room to stand who was experiencing muscle spasms in their back to the left of their right shoulder blade. I didn't think about how many people might be experiencing this feeling. I was just hoping there was one person so I could pray and my back would feel better. Thirty people stood up, so I invited them forward for prayer and the Lord met them. The ministry team joined us in praying for everyone, but my back pain went away as I prayed for the first person.

There were also deeper issues the Lord revealed for each person, but they were willing to receive prayer because of the precise description of their pain. God lovingly let them know that He knew about their physical and emotional pain and wanted to take it away.

Spontaneous Utterance

A seventh way of hearing God is through spontaneous utterance, which simply means that you blurt out something that hits the person like an arrow. It is not just someone's inability to concentrate or wait their turn in a conversation. It is the Lord directly saying something in a way to jolt the person to response. This occurred for me one day when two dating college students came up to me after chapel to ask for prayer. After they asked the question, I immediately blurted out, "No,

I won't pray for you until you stop having sex!" Momentarily, all three of us stood there looking at each other, and in my head I was screaming, "Oh my word, I can't believe I just said that!" The couple put their heads down and said, "You're right. We want to repent of this sin." They both prayed a prayer of repentance. Then I prayed for them. I had no way of knowing this was their situation. It came out of my mouth before I realized what had happened. God wanted them to bring it into the light so they could have accountability in their relationship.

Prophetic Parallel

An eighth way of hearing God is through prophetic parallel. Sometimes the person you encounter reminds you of someone else and as you apply what you know about your friend or relative to this situation, it aligns. My husband once prayed for a young lady who looked like his niece Kim. He kept opening and closing his eyes to look at her, because of the similarity.

He finally decided to go with it and asked her if her name was Kim, the same as his niece. The young lady said yes. Are you a schoolteacher? The same as his niece. She said yes. He went on to pray about her creativity. After they finished praying, the young lady told Ron that she was struggling with quitting her job to write children's books. Shortly after we moved to New York, we received a children's picture book in the mail with a letter in the front from Kimberly, thanking my husband for praying for her and saying she believed her book was part of the fulfillment of what he prayed for her that day.

YOU TOO?

Oftentimes after hearing these descriptions and stories, people relate that they have also had similar experiences, but they didn't know it was God. It will take faith for us to act on what we hear. Fear of being wrong often holds us back from praying, but if done in love with the goal of the person to feel God's love, our mistakes are usually forgiven.

What if our praying reveals something the person has never told anyone and they are drawn closer to God? Isn't it worth the risk? Humbly offer what you hear to the person. If it's God, the person will know it. God is good, and He wants to have an intimate relationship that involves speaking to Him, listening, and obeying His word to us.

Nine Scriptural Tests for Hearing God's Voice

These nine tests from the Bible help us determine if what we are hearing is from God.

Strength, Encouragement, Comfort

The first test asks the question, does the word we hear strengthen, encourage, and comfort us as I Corinthians 14:3 directs? Even a difficult word will accomplish these three things. Hearing we need to cut off a toxic relationship that impedes our relationship with God is the Lord. We know deep down that the relationship is not healthy, but we've conveniently ignored all signs and stayed in it. The Lord has now made it clear to us that we need to cut off the relationship, and we are strengthened, encouraged, and comforted to know that God will be with us as we walk it out.

Agreement with Scripture

The second test asks the question, is the word we hear in agreement with Scripture? "All Scripture is God-breathed and is useful for teaching, rebuking, correcting and training in righteousness" (II Tim. 3:16a). The Scripture is a primary way in which God speaks, so anything outside it must align with the Word of God. This does not mean that every word can have a chapter and verse to back it, but the ways of God are also seen throughout Scripture so there is understanding and guidance of God through the overarching themes of Scripture. God will not tell a person to do something that is opposed to His written Word, because God doesn't contradict Himself.

Exalt Jesus

The third test for God's voice is does this word exalt Jesus? In John 16:14, Jesus is talking about the Holy Spirit when He says, "He (Holy Spirit) will glorify me (Jesus) because it is from me that He will receive what he will make known to you." Jesus goes on to say that "all that belongs to the Father is mine. That is why I said the Spirit will receive from me what he will make known to you" (v. 15). The purpose of relationship with God is to hear his words—words are from the Holy Spirit to exalt Jesus for the glory of the Father. Revelation 19:10 reads, "For it is the Spirit of prophecy that bears testimony to Jesus."

Good Fruit

The fourth test is, does the word have good fruit? We will never know the outcome until we act on what we hear. It isn't enough just to hear it. Hearing and obedience go hand in hand. It takes trust that what you are hearing is from God. Then it takes faith to apply that to your own life or speak it out to someone else. Luke 11:11–13 reads,

> "Which of you fathers, if your son asks for a fish, will give him a snake instead? Or if he asks for an egg, will give him a scorpion? If you, then though you are evil, know how to give good gifts to your children, how much more will your Father in heaven give the Holy Spirit to those who ask him!"

God is not going to give us something to hurt us, so we can trust Him in the process. We must learn what God sounds like, and one of the ways we can tell it is Him is by the fruit that is produced. Is it good fruit or bad fruit? Does a person feel loved by God, or do they feel judged, belittled, criticized, or hopeless?

Accurate Prediction

The fifth scriptural test for God's voice is if the word predicts a future event, does the event happen? Deuteronomy 18:22 reads, "If what a prophet proclaims in the name of the Lord does not take place or come true, that is a message the Lord has not spoken. That prophet has spoken presumptuously. Do not be afraid of him." It is important that a person is both credible and accurate. First Thessalonians 5:19–21 cautions the reader by saying, "Do not put out the Spirit's fire; do not treat prophecies with contempt. Test everything. Hold on to the good." Not every single word given will be 100 percent accurate 100 percent of the time, because we are fallible human beings; however, that doesn't mean we should throw out all prophecies, quench the Spirit's fire, and despise all words. We need to test everything, so we hold on to the good, ponder what we have heard, and wait for the Lord to reveal more to us so over time, we can piece together what He is saying.

Turns You Toward or Away From God?

The sixth test for hearing God's voice is, are people turned toward God or away from Him? Deuteronomy 13:1–3a reads,

> "If a prophet, or one who foretells by dreams, appears among you and announces to you a sign or wonder, and if the sign or wonder spoken of takes place, and the prophet says, 'Let us follow other gods' (gods you

have not known) 'and let us worship them,' you must not listen to the words of that prophet or dreamer."

The voice of God will draw people to Himself, not to another human being. The apostle Paul extensively charges Timothy in II Timothy 3:1–5 to beware of the following kinds of people:

"There will be terrible times in the last days. People will be lovers of themselves, lovers of money, boastful, proud, abusive, disobedient to their parents, ungrateful, unholy, without love, unforgiving, slanderous, without self-control, brutal, not lovers of the good, treacherous, rash, conceited, lovers of pleasure rather than lovers of God—having a form of godliness but denying its power. Have nothing to do with such people."

Sometimes the person giving the word is simply immature. It is easy to ignore their word by judging their looks, their age, their experience, and even the delivery of the word itself; however, we need to be careful with this, because sometimes God offends our pride and gives the word to us through someone we don't like or respect. That doesn't mean the word is wrong and we should reject it. We need to be wise and discerning and align the spoken words with the written words of God. The voice of God draws people to Himself.

Freedom or Bondage?

The seventh test for God's voice is does the word produce freedom or bondage? Paul wrote in Romans 8:14–16,

For those who are led by the Spirit of God are the children of God. The Spirit you received does not make you slaves, so that you live in fear again; rather, the Spirit you received brought about your adoption to sonship.

And by him we cry, "Abba, Father." The Spirit himself testifies with our spirit that we are God's children.

As a son or daughter, we have full rights and privileges of our father's inheritance. All that belongs to God now belongs to us too. "It is for freedom that Christ has set us free. Stand firm, then, and do not let yourselves be burdened again by a yoke of slavery" (Gal. 5:1). Paul warns the reader to stand firm and not let yourselves be burdened again. Staying free requires believing the truth about who we are and what we've been given—this is by grace through faith.

Life or Death?

The eighth test for God's voice is, does the word produce life or death? The letter of the law produces death because of the impossibility to keep it. It is harsh, judgmental, and critical. The voice of God produces life to those who hear it, giving hope and healing to all who are willing to receive it. Jesus said, "The Spirit gives life; the flesh counts for nothing. The words I have spoken to you—they are full of the Spirit and life" (Jn. 6:63).

> Staying free requires believing the truth about who we are and what we've been given.

Witness of Holy Spirit

The final test for God's voice is, does the Holy Spirit bear witness that the word is true? Jesus told his disciples, "When he, the Spirit of truth, comes, he will guide you into all the truth. He will not speak on his own; he will speak only what he hears, and he will tell you what is yet to come" (Jn. 16:13). This brings assurances to know that the Holy Spirit will guide us into all truth.

GOD'S VOICE OR SATAN'S VOICE?

So how do we know we are hearing God and not the enemy? The voice of our enemy, Satan, is a vague, condemning voice that leads to feeling shame and despair, and produces fear in us. The Bible is clear that "there is now no condemnation for those who are in Christ Jesus" (Rom. 8:1). The voice of the enemy is an accusing voice that taunts, harasses, and torments us.

The convicting voice of the Holy Spirit is specific, is restorative, leads to repentance, gives hope, and produces love and peace. God's voice provides solutions and freedom.

It is important to distinguish these voices, because many people attribute to God the voice of the accuser. That voice is NOT God! The voice of God always shows us the way out of trouble by the empowering presence of the Holy Spirit within us.

Whether sitting alone to listen to God or listening when praying for a friend, faith and action are needed in the process. Humbly receive the word you heard, weigh it against Scripture, and then humbly and lovingly act on what you heard. In this way, you will figure out what the Lord sounds like. God will make himself heard. Wait for Him.

Mirror Moment

Take a moment to recall the ways God has spoken to you in the past. Which of the eight ways described in this chapter have you heard from the Lord (word, phrase, picture, vision, song, Scripture, spontaneous utterance, or prophetic parallel)? Take a moment and tell the Lord you will begin to act on the things you see, sense, feel, or hear from Him.

OBSTACLE: NOISE (OUTER AND INNER)

What are some ways the enemy is obstructing your ability to hear God? An obstacle to hearing God is both the outer noise and inner noise of our lives. Outer noise consists of physical sounds that distract us and inhibit our hearing. Inner noise consists of unrestrained thoughts that ruminate in our minds in the form of negative self-talk and unchecked feelings that stir in our soul, producing anxiety or unrest.

Our willingness to live with the chaos of noise determines our potential for self-awareness and intimacy. It's easier to yell over the noise than stop it and face the clamor within ourselves. Hearing God requires that we stop the noise and allow what's inside to bubble to the surface for us to identify it and give it to the Lord. His gentle voice then instructs us what to do with our findings.

CREATING A SACRED PLACE

Choosing a place within our home to listen is important. We can obviously meet with God anywhere, but a designated space in our home becomes the place where we regularly encounter the Lord and create memories together, in the same way that spouses and best friends have favorite places unique to their relationship.

Inner noise is a bit more difficult to quiet. Once the outer noise ceases, it takes time to discipline the mind to momentarily release work responsibilities and relationship issues as well as to identify negative feelings of unresolved pain. Our distorted view of God also plays a part in our distancing. Recognition of how we view God is vital for us to be able to draw near to him.

If we think he is angry or frustrated with us, we will only come so close. It's hard to be intimate with someone we fear, because we are hoping our behavior doesn't set him off to turn his wrath toward us. If we think God is emotionally distant or absent, we won't bother to come close because we self-protect against being abandoned yet again from someone who is supposed to care for us.

Threat of disappointment keeps us emotionally distant from God. Coupled with thoughts that He has more important things to do than listen to us gives us reason to believe He won't come. The quiet is sometimes avoided, not for fear of what God will say, but for fear that He won't say anything, or worse yet, He won't even show up. Our view of God, no matter how distorted, must be revealed to us, so we can work through the lies and press in with truth.

Take a moment and list three positive adjectives and three negative adjectives that describe your father. In what way(s) do you tend to view God with these same characteristics? Find a trusted mentor, friend, counselor, or pastor to help you process how you view God. Begin to look for Bible verses that describe God as loving and kind. Write some of these verses on Post-it notes or index cards and put them in key places in your home to read regularly. Memorizing some of them as the Lord directs you will replace your distorted view of God with an accurate view of Him found in the Bible. God is for you and nothing will ever be able to separate you from His love (Rom 8:31–39).

THE WAY THROUGH: DISCIPLINE OF LISTENING PRAYER

Listening to God takes time, attention, and energy. In the kingdom of God, intimacy and authority are developed by going ALONE into the closet, shutting the door, and praying to the Father, who we cannot see (Mt. 6:6). It goes against everything we've ever thought or been taught about warfare, because in a battle, no one goes alone. We stay together, work together, and particularly watch the back of your battle buddy. In the kingdom of God, there is a different way of doing things. Jesus is our battle buddy. The breakthrough we need is revealed in the presence of the Lord with Jesus on one side interceding and the Holy Spirit on the other side groaning when we have run out of words. In this vulnerable place *with* our God, breakthrough is revealed.

BREAKTHROUGH IS SEALED BY THE STRATEGY OF GOD.

When we figure out *what* the Lord is saying to us, we then must determine what we do with His words. What is the Lord's strategy for this situation? Breakthrough is sealed by the strategy of God, but unless we draw near to hear from Him, we can easily miss the way He wants to do something. We go into the closet to get away from the noise, the distractions, and the opinions all around us.

There are plenty of people to draw from with a simple search on Google or YouTube. Suggestions or words of wisdom abound from "successful" people we admire. But there is one specific solution for our situation that has been perfectly crafted because of who we are and where we are. There is a *now word strategy* straight from the heart of God for us that surpasses anything another person could offer. God's strategy for you has been intentionally chosen for this exact time and mission. It is good and wise to glean from others, but our specific orders for each situation come only from Him. He never does the same thing twice, so we become comfortable with ambiguity as we live in the present to fulfill today's plan in the precise way He gave it. Yes, breakthrough is sealed by the strategy of God.

BREAKTHROUGH IS ACTIVATED BY OUR OBEDIENCE.

Breakthrough is also activated by our obedience. It is when we come out of the secret place with clear directives that the breakthrough begins as we obey what He gave us. It's one thing to hear from God, but then we must come out and act. It's okay that it's never been done this way before. God is the One who came up with the plan, so He will guide us through all the details to fulfill it. "And your Father who sees what is done in secret, will reward you" (Mt. 6:6).

Our reward is His presence with us to do what He asked in the secret place. If He wants something done a certain way, He is going to remove every obstacle, provide every resource, and sustain us to accomplish that purpose. We simply say yes to Him and move in that direction. The breakthrough comes as we move in obedience.

The only way is *through*, so we need to go into the closet, shut the door, and pray to our Father who we cannot see and let Him show us the way through. Breakthrough is revealed in the presence of the Lord, sealed by the strategy of God, and activated by our obedience. He will reveal Himself to us as *we* need. Our strategy will be unique to each of us, but we need to listen and obey. Our breakthrough will come.

PRACTICE: KEEP COMING

Set aside time again today to enter the closet and seek the Lord. Practicing these stillness moments may only produce an occasional nugget from the Lord. Write it down, keep showing up, and wait for the next piece.

DISCUSSION QUESTIONS

1. *What thoughts come to mind when you try to pray?*

2. *Share with the group a story of how you hear the Lord?*

3. *Which scriptural test brings you the most comfort?*

4. *What is your loudest inner noise that interrupts your intimacy with God?*

5. *For what reason do you give up praying for breakthrough in your life?*

6. *Take time to pray for each other in your group, listening for the Lord as described in this chapter.*

Chapter 8.

CHARACTER: WHO I AM WHEN NO ONE ELSE SEES ME

The moral and ethical qualities developed within us as we heed the Father's directive, "Others may, you may not."[40]

Who are you when no one else is looking? Character is who we are when no one else sees us. It is not determined by one decision; it is the summation of many. Time is a factor in character development because it cannot happen quickly. It is a very slow process that happens one decision at a time, choice by choice by choice. The culmination of these choices determines if character is good or bad. Inner moral and ethical

---

[40] Ron Walborn. My husband received this Word from the Lord while praying. He shared it in a Personal Spiritual Formation Class lecture, Nyack College, spring, 2000.

qualities are distinctive to the individual, with each person living within a range of comfortability with each decision.

Family values shape our thinking and actions for what is right and wrong, good and bad, and acceptable and unacceptable behavior. It is in this setting where we develop our moral and ethical range of comfortability to abide by the rules. Consequences of actions are often a deterrent to wrongful behavior for most people, but for some, no consequence will sway them from doing what they want. Rather than stop the behavior, they go underground and continue the behavior in secrecy.

INTERNAL MORAL COMPASS

Ongoing choices of engagement in harmful activities can produce life-threatening results that make recovery difficult. It is this internal moral and ethical compass from which decisions are made to either align with rules or to rebel and do our own thing. Society is structured for people to align with laws to provide safety, equality, and stability for all people. People who choose to live outside the moral and ethical codes of society either live on the margins of society or are imprisoned for their immoral and unethical behavior. There is incongruency between their internal compass and the external expectations of society. Traits like honesty, integrity, and trustworthiness form within an individual as a result of good choices. A continuation of bad choices also forms character that produces a lying, cheating, and untrustworthy person.

In the movie *Annapolis*, a character named Estrada was ordered to shower every two hours for six weeks. He faithfully set his alarm throughout the night to comply with the order. The last night of the requirement, Estrada's alarm went off and he rolled over and went back to sleep. Both of his roommates noticed, but only Lou told him to confess to his commanding officer. Estrada's attitude was, "So what. It's only a shower." Lou replied, "It's not about the shower. It's about the very first thing we learned here—to tell the truth." Lou turned in Estrada to their commanding officer, and Estrada

> Good character comes from an intrinsic motivation to do the right thing simply because it is the right thing.

was discharged from the Naval Academy. It was a harsh outcome, but the military follows an honor code. Policies and rules effectively regulate outward behavior, but it doesn't mean inward agreement.

Good character comes from an intrinsic motivation to do the right thing simply because it is the right thing. Do you always do the right thing, even when no one is looking? Fear of getting caught or fear of punishment may deter unacceptable behavior, but it doesn't get to the root of why the person acted out in the first place. Individuals become calculating in finding the loophole in the rule they seek to break, arguing about the technicality of its wording if they are found in violation. Thinking of others doesn't come into their minds, because they want to do it and will do it regardless of anyone else. The response, "It's not hurting anybody else" is often used to defend one's thinking and actions. Guidance and mentorship can provide support to people in the midst of character-forming choices.

REPENTANCE

King David penned these words to God after his adultery with Bathsheba: "Surely you desire truth in the inner parts; you teach me wisdom in the inmost place." The choices we make in this inmost place are where character is either developed or delayed. Speaking the truth when a lie would work better, fulfilling work responsibilities when everyone else lets things slide, and giving back the extra money the cashier handed us are examples of choices that form good character. No one else sees and knows the struggle of choice, except us and God. We can get away with it outwardly, but inwardly it will eat at us. This is the place where choosing truth brings freedom. Listening to the voice of the Holy Spirit is our guide in these choices. His voice is sometimes a tiny whisper saying, **"Others may, you may not."** Such direction is ours alone to follow. No comparison, no negotiating, and no cry for fairness—God Himself has told us no and that is enough.

There is freedom that comes in admitting we are not okay and need help. Simple acknowledgement of wrongdoing and bringing it into the light is a great start. There is something powerful in saying it out loud. "If we confess our sins, he is faithful and just to forgive us our sins and purify us from all unrighteousness" (I Jn. 1:9). Hearing ourselves confess the sin disarms the shameful hold. The choice is whether or not we will confess our sins—IF.

Our release and freedom are contingent upon our choice to humble ourselves and agree with our wrongdoing through confession. Confession within a safe community allows others to speak truth and offer love to us in the midst of our pain. "Confess your sins to each other and pray for each other so that you may be healed" (James 5:16). You don't have to walk this journey alone. Your community is there to listen to your confession and pray for your healing.

Repentance differs from confession in that repentance is a decision to turn away and go in the opposite direction, while confession is an admission of wrongdoing. Many people are able to admit what they have done, but there is no remorse or desire for change. Confession of this kind is simply a catharsis—a release of emotion by speaking it out. Many people on the spiritual journey are immature because they confess their sins, but refuse to repent of their sins. There is a big difference between admitting it and repenting of it.

One of the roles of the Holy Spirit in our lives is to convict of sin, and when He convicts, there is a choice to be made to listen to Him and repent or ignore Him and turn away. Each refusal to listen and repent hardens our heart a little bit more until it becomes like a rock. The kindness of God leads to repentance, because we remember that we are loved and that in our confession, He is faithful and just to forgive us. We have a choice to humble ourselves and receive forgiveness or stay in our pride and harden our hearts.

THE CONSEQUENCE OF A BAD CHOICE

When I was a senior in high school, our government class went to the state capitol in Augusta, Maine, for an overnight trip. We stayed in a hotel and my friend invited me to another room where people were hanging out. I knew people would be drinking and smoking pot, but I was curious about such activities, since I had never been to a party. So I said I would go for a little while—just to see what it was like. I walked into the hotel room, and there were probably twenty-five people in there. The room was filled with loud music, smoke (which I came to learn was the smell of marijuana), and beer. We were only eighteen years old. I sat down on the bed by the phone, and every warning signal inside me was screaming danger!

I stood up to leave when my teacher opened the door. We were busted. She glanced around the room, and her eyes remained on me with a look I will never forget. With that gaze, I heard, "Wow, I never expected to see you in here." There was nothing to say. I hadn't had any alcohol or smoked anything. I had only been in the room for three minutes, but I was in the room. I was guilty by association. For the first time, I understood the concept on a whole new level. All I could think was how my dad was going to kill me.

Thankfully the teacher left my name off the list of people in the room that night that was handed in to the principal's office. Needless to say, the school never again made that trip with students. The worst part of the story is that I lied to my dad when he asked if I knew anything about it. I left out the part of the story about being in the room when the teacher walked in. I simply said I had been in the room, but left because I knew what everyone was doing was wrong.

My rationalization in my head was that I was on my way out. I was going to leave. One more minute and I would have met the teacher in the hallway instead of the room. The story was close enough to the truth. Close enough to the truth—is a lack of character. Partial truth is still a lie. I never told my father the truth. I just lived with the guilt and shame of my lie, hoping he never found out. My curiosity wasn't wrong. My choice to lie and stick to my lie was wrong.

ADAM I AND ADAM II

In his book *The Road to Character*, David Brooks wrote of the opposing sides of human nature found in all of us. He described these conflicts as Adam I and Adam II. Adam I represented drives for external validation through career success and material accomplishment, and Adam II is driven by higher moral virtues, such as the desire to be a good person, to love well, and to sacrifice for the needs of others. These drives are often in conflict in our lives with Adam I wanting to conquer the world and Adam II wanting to obey a calling to serve the world.

If a person only develops Adam I, he will lack character. It is our acts of love and service that form good character. Developing Adam II is where we need the power of God to empower us to desire to help others. Our drives of conquering and calling unite as the character of Christ is formed in us to reach a hurting world.

Mirror Moment

How do people see you? If you were to ask a former teacher, someone from your church, a coach, or your mother to describe your character, what would they say about you? Write down what you would want them to say about you. In what ways, if any, are there discrepancies between your behavior and what you would want them to say about you?

GOD'S TESTIMONY

Acts 13:22 reads, "After removing Saul, he made David their king. God testified concerning him: 'I have found David son of Jesse, a man after my own heart; he will do everything I want him to do.'" How is it that God testified of David? He must have chosen David for something we cannot see. We look at David's story with Bathsheba, the murder of her husband Uriah, and the cover-up to follow and conclude that David's character disqualified him as a godly man. God chose David as a man after His heart because He saw something different in David.

The formation of character is a heart issue that only God can see.

When Samuel anointed David king at the age of fifteen in I Samuel 16:7, God said he doesn't look at the things people look at.

People look at the outward appearance, but the Lord looks at the heart. The formation of character is a heart issue that only God can see. David was a man who desired to be close to God, and only God could see His heart to know that about him.

In reading David's story of adultery, lying, deception, and murder, it is an obvious conclusion that David is not a man of good character, but God thought otherwise. God's statement of finding a man after his own heart gives us insight as to what God is looking for in a person when he says, "He [David] will do everything I want him to do." God is not looking for perfection, rather a heart that desires to obey Him and do whatever He wants.

When David was confronted with his sin by the prophet Nathan, he repented. He didn't just confess his sins. He repented. He turned and went in the other direction, and God testified about him that he would do anything God wanted him to do. This offers hope to us as followers that when we sin, grace will be extended to us in the midst of our confession and repentance. We will still need to live out the consequences of our sin, as David did, but grace flows down and covers us.

OBSTACLE: TEMPTATION

What is your biggest obstacle or stumbling block? One of the biggest obstacles to character formation is temptation to do our own thing. We want to be our own god. We don't say that out loud, because it doesn't sound spiritual, but in essence, we want to be our own boss and do our own thing. We don't want others impinging on our freedom of speech, freedom of thought, and freedom of behavior.

Our moral and ethical code is unique to each of us, so adherence to a standard outside ourselves is necessary to avoid implosion. If left to us, our selfish choices would run us into the ground. Our passions demand instant gratification, and delayed gratification requires a conscious choice. Our will is strong, but we choose to surrender to the will of another. We think we know what we want, but later are so thankful we didn't get what we wanted, because it would have been terrible for us. God knows us better than we know ourselves, so we are able to willingly give him access to our lives by saying yes to His plan.

PERSEVERANCE

Journeying with Jesus means we get to take His hand, keep in step with the Spirit, go at His pace, and do the things He wants us to do. We still want our own way, but soon discover that God is good and can be trusted. With this as the foundation, we can surrender to His plan and don't have to keep rebelling to get our own way. A good God who loves us brings good things into our lives and works all things together for our good. Keeping track of God's goodness in our lives, even in the little things, encourages us to put our faith in Him and keep trusting Him when things get hard.

Are you letting God use these choices to shape you? It is in these very choices where perseverance is developed in us, ultimately forming godly character. Testing reveals what we are like inside and often comes in the form of temptation. What choice will we make in the midst of the option? Which way will we go? We weigh our decision, knowing there will be a price to pay. We wrestle in our mind if the consequence of our choice will be worth committing the act.

Paul encourages the Corinthians by telling them "no temptation has overtaken you except what is common to mankind. And God is faithful; he will not let you be tempted beyond what you can bear. But when you are tempted, he will also provide a way out so that you can endure it" (I Cor. 10:13). God is not trying to tease us with trials. He is showing us that trials reveal who we are on the inside and afford us opportunity to act and look more like Jesus. The Holy Spirit within us will help us endure the temptation and show us the way out. It may not be a quick fix and pain may be involved, but He is with us every step of the way. Perseverance is what produces character.

THE WAY THROUGH: DISCIPLINE OF SUBMISSION

As Westerners, submission may be one of the most difficult spiritual disciplines of engagement due to its requirement of all that we are. Why? Because no one wants to be told what to do by another person. Submission is wholehearted agreement to voluntarily come under the authority of another person in unreserved obedience. Submission is often portrayed as a pushing down or lording over attitude to force the person to come under authority.

The biblical meaning of submission is an attitude to come under someone to lift them up with honor. These are two very different pictures. One is oppressive and one is revering. In both attitudes, the person submitting comes under the authority, but the attitude is very different. If wives are to submit to husbands and God with the first attitude, resistance and rebellion, even if only inward, will be present in the one expected to submit, because love is absent.

Biblical submission with the second attitude will be out of love and adoration as husbands and God are lifted up and honored for who they are. Paul addresses husbands and wives to "submit to one another out of reverence for Christ" (Eph. 5:21). With this view of submission, we are happy to lift up and honor each other.

In American culture, we pride ourselves in fighting for the rights of mankind. So much blood has been shed for equal rights, why would we now relinquish those rights to subject ourselves to another person? The answer lies in our motivation. For any reason other than love, submission is a duty or obligation. Love provides the intrinsic motivation to willingly relinquish our rights. Only love can cause people to give their lives.

> Only love can cause people to give their lives.

For men and women entering military service, there is an expectation that love of country is expected above marriage and family! Entering into this relationship means that devotion is pledged and expected at any cost—even death.

Soldiers are trained to lay down their lives for their country. With an all-in attitude, forward movement is the only option. Hesitancy will not exist once an order is given. Action will be swift and thorough to fulfill the given command. Outside a military setting, a person displaying allegiance like this would be called a fanatic and accused of being a member of a cult to offer such dedication.

The inference of James 4:7 to "submit to God, resist the devil and he will flee from you" is that if we don't submit to God and resist the devil, he (the devil) will not leave us alone, seeking to get us to surrender to him. It's a decisive choice. We either choose God and His way or we choose the devil and his way. People don't like to think of this as black and white.

We want to customize our relationship with God by picking and choosing things that make us comfortable and serve our wants and needs. We want to obey if it suits us and do our own thing if it doesn't. We want to keep our options open.

We find it hard to call doing our own thing disobedience, because we don't want to be seen in a bad light. Doing our own thing simply reveals our desire to reserve a piece of our heart for ourselves, when God has asked for all. All means all. There is no way around it.

HOLY COURTESY

Leanne Payne wrote that "obedience is the 'holy courtesy' required for entering into the divine relationship."[41] She goes on to say that we "do not fail in obedience through lack of love,

[41] Leanne Payne, *Real Presence: The Christian Worldview of C. S. Lewis as Incarnational Reality* (Wheaton: Crossway, 1979), 24–25.

but have lost love because we have not attempted obedience."[42] If we choose to believe in Jesus and devote our lives to Him, we have to accept the terms of the offer. It is non-negotiable as to its conditions. "If anyone receives Jesus and believes in his name, they are given the right to become children of God" (Jn. 1:12). Therefore, the other side is that if anyone chooses *not* to receive Jesus and believe in his name, they are *not* given the right to become children of God. Either-or. Cut and dried. It really is that simple. Søren Kierkegaard wrote, "It is not a person's words, but an individual's life, that is the best picture of faith."[43]

Even in stating it this way, annoyance is stirred up in some readers when they see only two options. Even more is the aversion to someone stating that if we don't do it God's way, we don't get to be his children. As a culture, we have moved so far away from absolute truth, it appears abrasive to make a direct statement.

We have adopted our culture's embrace of relative truth, believing that my truth is my truth and your truth is your truth. Carrying over such a view into our relationship with God, we expect the same freedom to believe what we want and live as we please. Again, such a viewpoint reveals what was previously stated that we want relationship with God on our own terms.

The way of the kingdom is submission to the will of the king. All subjects in the kingdom align to His will and His way. It is your choice. Your choices matter, and just like me,

---

[42] Payne, *Real Presence*, 81.
[43] Søren Kierkegaard, *Concluding Unscientific Postscript* (Princeton: Princeton University Press, 1941), 31.

you will live with the consequences of those choices. The big question that remains is are you all-in? Yes or no? I know I am, and I hope that through this journey, you have found the freedom and the courage to be all-in too.

PRACTICE: OTHERS MAY, YOU MAY NOT

"Others may, you may not." Think about this statement as if the Lord were speaking it directly to you. What are some directives you have sensed from the Holy Spirit that you have shrugged off as too demanding? They may be things He has asked you to do or things He has asked you to stop doing. Write out a prayer of intention telling the Lord that you do hear Him and choose to obey. Be specific.

DISCUSSION QUESTIONS

1. *Why does it take so long for good character to be formed in us?*

2. *Share a story of your poor choice of character. What did you learn from this experience?*

3. *What is the expectation about telling the truth in your family and neighborhood? (Some people call this snitching.)*

4. *What do you think or feel when you hear that God testified about David after knowing the depths of darkness in David?*

5. *What is your view on submission?*

6. *Describe your thoughts or feelings about absolute surrender to God.*

7. *Give us an example of when you have sensed the Holy Spirit's prompting that others may, you may not.*

Afterword

WHERE DO I GO FROM HERE?

Our journey has come to an end for now, but it's certainly not over. I am so proud of you! You have done a great job facing the places within you that have held you back from the closeness with God that you have desired. The closer you get to God, the more you realize how much you don't know Him. There is an endless abundance of more to know, more love to experience, and more moments to be with Him, while listening and enjoying His presence.

LIVING FREE

You have emptied some things from your backpack that have weighed you down your whole life. The good news is that you never have to pick them up again. You have also been given helpful suggestions to tend to your wounds along the way. Ignoring the pain won't make it go away. You must stop, take off your shoes and socks, look at your injuries, and figure out what needs to be done for healing to occur. You weren't made to limp through life. You were made to walk at God's pace and in step with the Spirit.

You have found out on this journey that knowing the right thing and doing the right thing are two very different things. You must apply what you know to your life, and that is always the hard part. Angst produces opportunity for change. You can dull the angst with noise, or you can get quiet and see what's causing it.

You have taught yourself to suck it up and push through the pain. Those were the old ways you survived. On this journey, you have discovered that naming your pain and giving it the proper care it needs brings healing. Ointment and Band-Aids won't do any good for a pulled tendon or muscle. That requires rest. You have learned to give yourself grace and listen to your needs. Well done.

Throughout our journey together, you dismantled your mask, allowing the real you to come out. As you did, you found that God and others love the real you, and it still feels overwhelming as you think of it. Get used to it. That is part of the beauty of God's healing presence. Once you are free, you don't care who knows the pain you've tried to hide your whole life. Shame's hooks have been released and you see yourself in the light of God's grace and limitless love that is continuously extended to you.

BRING OTHERS ALONG

God's love is life-giving and compels you to want to tell others and bring them along on this adventure. Yes, indeed! Tell your family and friends what God has shown you and invite them onto the trail. You know what you're talking about and you can show them the tips you've learned along the way.

Remember that each person's journey is personal and their pace may be different than yours. Let them go at their own pace with God. Instead of rushing them, encourage them about what is ahead and rest with them when they need to stop to tend to a blister, eat a snack, or take a drink. Soon they, too, will become comfortable with voicing their pain and need as you share with them your story. Stay with those fellow travelers who will continue to walk with you in this newly found freedom. Choose wisely. Don't choose those who will encourage you to go back to faking it and pretending the pain isn't there.

It has been my delight to walk with you. Let me know when you want to go back to one of the parts of the trail, and I'll be right there with you. I'll cheer you on and remind you to pause again for Mirror Moments so the Lord can show you what's going on inside you. It gets easier every time, and eventually you will revisit parts of the trail that you recall as being the most painful, and you will see the sting is gone. That's when you really know you have grown and received healing.

God's promise to you is "I will never leave you, nor forsake you" (Joshua 1:5). He's always with you, and will not just carry your bag for you when you get tired. He will carry you! Let Him. This is the love and intimacy you have longed for. Receive it and give it away to other hurting travelers. Can you really get close to God? Now you know the answer! You absolutely can! See you on the trail!

About the Author

WANDA WALBORN is a professor, speaker, and leader who has served at Nyack College for the last twenty years. Training, equipping, and releasing strong leaders to advance the kingdom of God is her passion.

During her time at Nyack as Director of Spiritual Formation, Wanda was instrumental in changing the spiritual ethos of Nyack by creating the Introduction to Spiritual Formation class curriculum, which all new incoming students take their first semester on campus. Coordinating class topics with chapel speaker topics afforded students the opportunity to hear and respond to the voice of God in their lives.

Wanda now serves full-time as Associate Professor of Spiritual Formation at Nyack College and Alliance Theological Seminary. Wanda is a conference and retreat speaker for multiple age groups and has mentored many emerging leaders over the years.

Wanda also leads Empower, a certificate program for women, partnering with the Metropolitan District of the Christian and Missionary Alliance and Alliance Theological Seminary to equip women for effective ministry. Please visit the website at www.empowerww.org.

Wanda received her B.S. in Education from Nyack College, a M.A. in Intercultural Studies from Alliance Theological Seminary, and D.Int.St. from Western Seminary in Portland, Oregon. Prior to her employment at Nyack College, Wanda was a church planter with her husband, a stay-at-home mother for their four children, and a reading curriculum developer for the Connecticut public school system.

To reach Wanda to speak at your event, contact her at
Wanda@walbornleadership.com
or at her website, **walbornleadership.com**.